SPRAWL AND PUBLIC SPACE
REDRESSING THE MALL

National Endowment for the Arts · Washington, DC

David J. Smiley editor
Mark Robbins series editor

Distributed by:
Princeton Architectural Press
37 East Seventh Street
New York, New York 10003

For a free catalog of books, call 1.800.722.6657.
Visit our web site at www.papress.com.

Design by M. Christopher Jones, The VIA Group LLC.

Printed and bound in the United States of America.

Library of Congress Cataloging-In-Publication
Data is available from the National Endowment
for the Arts.

ISBN 1-56898-376-X

NEA Series on Design

Other titles available in this series:

The Mayors' Institute:
Excellence in City Design

Schools for Cities:
Urban Strategies

University-Community
Design Partnerships:
Innovations in Practice

Your Town:
Mississippi Delta

Front cover:
A freeway sign reinforces
the sense of the shopping
center as an everyday
destination.

Contents

I
The Shopping Mall in Context: History and Politics

II
Case Studies

Foreword   1
William Ivey

Redressing the Mall   3
Mark Robbins

Towards an Open-   9
Minded Space
Robert Fishman

Addressing Redress   13
David Smiley

Suburban Life and   21
Public Space
Margaret Crawford

Civic Space   31
Benjamin R. Barber

Antidotes to Sprawl   37
Kevin Mattson

Repositioning the   49
Older Shopping Mall
Marilyn Jordan Taylor

Villa Italia,   51
Lakewood, Colorado
Mark Falcone

Two Malls,   53
Kettering, Ohio
Marilou W. Smith
Andrew Aidt

III
Redevelopment: Projects, Strategies, Research

IV
Development Issues and Problems

Urban Elements   58
Michael Rotondi

Three Landscapes   62
Glenn Allen

Mixed Uses, Mixed   68
Masses, Mixed Finances
Gary Handel

Reassembling the   72
Strip and Building
around the Big Box
Darren Petrucci

A Vertical Mixed-Use   74
Suburb
Lewis.Tsurumaki.Lewis

VMall: Vertical Density   76
SHoP

Design Competitions   78
as Catalysts
Rosalie Genevro

From Shopping Centers   81
to Village Centers
Richard B. Peiser
Will Fleissig
Martin Zogran

Roundtable: Obstacles   85
to Development
Mark Falcone
Joseph F. Reilly
Ron Sher
Donald R. Zuchelli
Benjamin R. Barber

Organizations   98

Bibliography   99

Image Credits   99

Contributors   100

Endnotes   104

Is there a way to energize these facilities, to reconceive them both as landscapes and as structures that can really reengage community?

—William Ivey

Foreword

William Ivey
Chairman, National Endowment for the Arts

This book is the result of the first direct collaboration between the
National Endowment for the Arts and the Woodrow Wilson
International Center for Scholars. Neighbors along Pennsylvania Avenue,
we are similarly dedicated to bringing together the leaders in our respec-
tive fields to serve the public good. An examination of the mall, sprawl,
and public space represents a natural meeting place for the special mission of the Endowment in design and the special mission of the Wilson
Center in public policy. This book represents a unique gathering of
expertise on a matter of crucial interest to the future of the American
built environment.

  The NEA is charged with nurturing our nation's creativity and
preserving our nation's living cultural heritage. Most recently we've talked
with Congress and citizen leaders around the country about the importance of placing creativity and cultural heritage at the center of
community and family life. That has the Endowment talking frequently
about the importance of arts education, in and out of school. But it also
has us interested in the built environment and the modified natural environment and the ways in which the quality of our engagement with
environment connects with our social patterns.

  Since the shopping center is a focal point in so many people's lives,
Redressing the Mall is timely and necessary. It is a synthesis of historical,

social, economic, and design studies that seek new ways of reusing what is among our country's most popular building types. This book not only asks that we look at the condition of the older shopping centers around our cities but that we look optimistically to find ways of making sure these shopping centers can once again contribute to our nation's social life. Especially important to this book are the many different points of view on the issue of sprawl and more particularly on the issue of troubled or abandoned shopping centers. This issue represents a very serious challenge and a real opportunity. Is there a way to energize these facilities, to reconceive them both as landscapes and as structures that can really re-engage community? This book concerns itself not only with what might be done, or what should be done, but what can be done and how it might be paid for. In my years in Nashville, Tennessee, as a director of the Country Music Foundation and the Country Music Hall of Fame, I participated in at least a half-dozen plans that attempted to shape the growth and redevelopment of different parts of the community of Nashville. Those plans unfortunately sit on shelves, and their recommendations have been ignored almost totally, not because of any lack of good will, but because the financing wasn't there, and thus the impulse was never there to move from planning through to execution. Too much was left to the good will of developers who couldn't afford to put in the fine elements of those plans. One crucial contribution of this book is that it attempts to synthesize the design element and the financial element as integral parts of the larger challenge to create public spaces.

Redressing the Mall

Mark Robbins
Director of Design, National Endowment for the Arts

The suburban shopping center might at first appear to be an unlikely object of scrutiny for the National Endowment for the Arts. In fact, the idea for this project emerged from our long-standing commitment to community planning and urban revitalization. *Redressing the Mall* complements two existing programs at the Arts Endowment that focus on American communities and design. The first, The Mayors' Institute on City Design, was originated in 1986. In six annual sessions the institute brings mayors together with architects, landscape architects, planners, and economic specialists to strategize the revitalization of their neighborhoods and downtowns. The second, Your Town, aims to foster a greater awareness of the ways that smaller communities can direct their own growth over the long term without eliminating the possibility of new development and change. Between these two programs, between downtown and the small town so to speak, lies the country's vast suburban landscape where most Americans live and work. Recognizing the unique history and scope of suburban development became the impetus for this project.

NEA Chairman Bill Ivey encouraged our examination of the commercial and social aspects of the suburbs and suggested, given the dimensions of the topic, the benefit of a specific focus. We chose to narrow the field to the proliferation of "dead malls," the older shopping centers that for a number of reasons had fallen into disuse. These commercial ventures no longer generate income for the municipality or for the developer, nor are they positive elements in the manmade landscape. Our primary goal in undertaking this project has therefore been to explore ways in which these sites could be reused and transformed into viable, productive centers often in places that have lost, or never really had, a community center. By exploring new approaches and innovative partnerships in economics, land use, planning, and design, we hope these often choice sites can become not only fiscally viable but positive assets to their communities.

We also hope this publication will foster a more serious examination of new models for making and using public space. Our culture is rapidly changing, and the nature of the public sphere has also changed dramatically over the years. For example, a recent headline in the *Washington Post*, "Hackers Attack Web Sites," framed the Internet as a kind of public realm, a concept that would have been meaningless five years ago. Often our preconceptions of place and space lag behind social and technological changes.

When we think about American cities, the image of a coherent urban center persists. Set at the other end of the spectrum, we often have a heroic image of rural America. Even our concept of what falls in between relies on a snapshot of suburban life idealized in the 1950s. But these views, frozen in a misty past, continue to influence decisions about the planning and design of the new suburban landscape. Most urban centers have long evidenced patterns of disinvestment and abandonment, depleted population and decayed building stock. Efforts to accommodate the automobile-based rules of the suburb created seas of surface parking anchored by a mere handful of significant, if isolated, towers. Today's American landscape is dominated by other patterns: cloverleaves of the interstate highways that girdle our cities, cul-de-sac office parks, and housing developments in isolated clusters. At times small fragments of the Jeffersonian grid show through as reminders of farm fields, the last remnant of the agrarian past. Yet, in this landscape, one still finds aspirations for something more, in the bucolic names of unremarkable strip centers, in new Victorian villages, and in the fiberglass barn siding of fast food

Typical patterns of development at the periphery of a city. Cul-de-sac developments, office parks, and highway arteries obscure the last remnants of farm fields and the national grid.

restaurants. All suggest the pull of memory and history as we gather to park and shop. A desire for continuity and familiarity continues to shape our ideals and the design of our environment.

More recently, other models of development have replaced older strips and shopping centers further out at the edges of existing development. In Columbus, Ohio, for example, a place called Easton Town Center, though built in 1999, looks at first glance like a traditional town. Easton is a recreation of a town square out of whole cloth with a seeming mix of building types and architectural styles. A hansom cab travels the abbreviated main street, inhabited by national retailers including J. Crew, Banana Republic, and Williams-Sonoma. The development currently sits like a commercial Oz in the middle of a cornfield.

Two issues are raised by this newer form of development. First, the nostalgic simulation of an older town preys on our desire for connection and community, though only as a marketing model. Second, and perhaps more problematic, is the fact that Easton Town Center sits in the tertiary ring, far out from the city center. The new roadways and infrastructure constructed to provide access to this development exacerbate sprawl, even as the new "Town Center" presents the appearance of an antidote.

Easton Town Center, a new commercial center created in the image of a historical town. On the left, the Easton Town Center "Code of Conduct."

While providing an image of civic comfort, Easton offers only a partial copy of urban public space. A comparison with a public market in Cincinnati, only two hours away, is instructive. The two places don't look very different until one comes across the Easton Town Center "Code of Conduct" and is reminded that Easton is not public space. Photo-IDs can be requested by security guards and "appropriate attire" is required. Unauthorized singing and dancing, the distribution of literature, and the "congregation of minors in groups larger than four" are expressly forbidden. (A photographer attempting to document the space, without authorization, was reprimanded by a guard and pointed in the direction of the decorative stanchion with the list of rules prominently displayed.)

The lesson for citizens and professionals is that Easton and other similar spaces are designed wholly to make us good consumers and to engage us in a fantasy, which includes the participation in what appears to be a public realm. Now, the ability to purchase fantasy and fulfillment is part of our birthright as Americans. What drives us psychically and socially, as well as in our shopping habits, often drives the market. But when this market-based fantasy is offered as the sole setting for community, we diminish the choices and opportunities for which we often pride ourselves. The reach of the market, however, is not completely limiting or determined. People are creative and will always appropriate space for their own, often unintended, uses. The design and control of space can deter or enhance our capacity to respond as individuals to the social and physical environment.

In this small publication, we hope to encourage other visions that enable communities to engage architecture and landscape in more complex and multifunctional ways than is usually the case. The work in this volume offers models for public spaces that encourage interaction. In addition, we hope that this material can show a variety of methods for the design and effective implementation of such models. We hope to encourage an idea of public that is perhaps best seen in one of the classic examples of American urban design: New York's Central Park. The park is a place where anyone can go, without an entry fee or minimum purchase; it is a place that encourages multiple activities, some commercial and some not; it is a place where one can stroll, play cards or baseball, exercise political speech in groups of all sizes, listen to music, buy a hot dog, or just stretch out and take a nap. For all types and ages of people, places like Central Park provide options. Great cities have always provided the space for their citizens to *be* in public, to register an individual presence in a collective environment.

As our culture changes, we need to envision other models for creating public space, forms of urbanism that don't quite exist yet. The suburbs will not all become dense in the same way as traditional urban centers, nor will the car spontaneously disappear; people will still want to be seen in public. This situation requires an innovative approach that recognizes the way we live, with cars, DVD players, and all. The hope is to accommodate social diversity, the pedestrian and the car, and satisfy our often conflicting desires for the suburban ease of big box shopping and for the liveliness of streets. This mix of uses may lead to new forms and terms that grow from the American context, requiring invention and subtlety in order to understand the complexity of the undertaking.

A stimulating new vision is called for: one that can help rescue the failing centers but also help them to be genuine places in the older areas of our spreading suburban environment. We need to develop a deeper sense of how to achieve these changes, and to work toward guidelines for action. This is the challenge for this book and for this project.

Acknowledgments

The conference on which this book is based—"Sprawl and Public Space: Redressing the Mall," held in February 2000—was framed within the first year of my tenure at the National Endowment for the Arts. Many people worked on the project and helped make the conference possible. I'd like to acknowledge my collaborator, the historian Robert Fishman, then a fellow at the Woodrow Wilson Center, our partners in this project. Fishman's 1987 *Bourgeois Utopias: The Rise and Fall of Suburbia* remains a central text in trying to understand the evolution of suburbia and its impact on American culture. I'd also like to thank Michael Lacey, Director of the American Program at the Wilson Center, for recognizing design and design discussion as integral parts of contemporary American culture. The Wilson Center's Susan Nugent and Ed Martini also provided invaluable coordination and assistance.

At the NEA, I'd like to recognize Chairman Bill Ivey for his insights and early support of this project; Karen Christensen, Deputy Chair, for her faith in this work; and Susan Begley, Design Specialist, who worked long and hard to make the conference a reality.

This publication has had an interesting course in coming to fruition. My thanks to David Smiley, editor, who has contributed great energy and insight in assembling and crafting the final form of this work. Jason Pearson, the first Graham Fellow in Federal Service at the NEA, has been invaluable in his spirited coordination of all our efforts and Kristina Alg, the second Graham Fellow, has worked to bring this project to completion. I would also like to thank Ann Bremner for her enlightened assistance with copy editing and M. Christopher Jones of The VIA Group for his exciting book design. I'm pleased that this book is appearing as part of the NEA series on design issued by the Princeton Architectural Press. At the press, Kevin Lippert and Jennifer Thompson offered generous support and guidance in finalizing the publication. Finally, great thanks are due to each participant in the symposium and to the contributors to this book. Their suggestions and perspectives have added to our collective view on a very complex field. The approaches that may be gleaned from this publication will, we hope, benefit us all.

Towards an Open-Minded Space

Robert Fishman
Taubman College of Architecture and Urban Planning,
University of Michigan

One central theme of political philosophy in recent years has been the importance of public space for the vitality of democracy. A democratic polity needs what the philosopher Michael Walzer has called "open-minded spaces," places where a wide variety of people can coexist, places where a wide variety of functions encourage unexpected activities, places whose multiple possibilities lead naturally to the communication that makes democracy possible. Americans used to show a remarkable talent in creating such places, but this talent has been lacking in first-ring suburbs, those developments built just after 1945. These places tend to be dominated by what Walzer has called "single-minded spaces," that is, spaces so rigorously defined for a single purpose that they exclude the liberating openness of genuine public space.

Despite the seeming ascendancy of single-minded spaces, an unexpected opportunity for the creation of public space has opened up in suburbs throughout the country. The changing economics of retailing has rendered obsolete many older, first-ring shopping malls, and these under-utilized or even dead malls are usually found in places without a traditional town center. The suburbs in which the malls are located are also experiencing demographic changes and aging of population, housing, and building stock. Boarded-up malls sit by the highway and function like billboards that say "Disinvest Here." Ultimately, the rise of dead malls undermines the communities in which they are located, fueling further disinvestment and sprawl, more distending and distortion of metropolitan communities.

Are there alternatives? Can dead malls be transformed from eye sores and financial liabilities to civic assets? Can their rebuilding become a sign that a positive cycle of rebuilding and renewal has replaced our terrible habit of abandonment? In other words, can these underutilized spaces be redesigned as open-minded spaces that can nurture a wide range of functions now neglected in most suburbs? Can the dead mall be transformed into the 21st-century version of the town square? Transforming the mall into a community gathering place might seem to contradict its very commercial essence. Walzer called the shopping center the epitome of single-mindedness, but this observation overlooks the complex and openly self-contradictory aspects of the form.

In part we need to recognize that the success of the shopping center comes out of the single-minded removal of the shopping function from the dense multifunctional downtown, and the substitution of this relatively simple fragment for what had been a complex whole. But when we look at the innovations that made this single-minded space possible—taking shopping to the suburbs, situating the stores in the center of vast parking lots, turning the stores inward towards a pedestrian space—we see the creation of what many observers have called a dream world of shopping. And this dream world has had a remarkable capacity to absorb new commercial, entertainment, and recreational functions, most notably the synthesis of the shopping center and the theme park. But is this open-minded space? Victor Gruen, the architect perhaps most responsible for the proliferation of shopping centers in the 1950s, believed they should be designed to "service civic, cultural and social community needs." In other words, malls can and must be open-minded spaces. Yet this transformation will be difficult to achieve, and there are many challenges.

First, a civic challenge. In suburbs where people are accustomed to driving directly to specific destinations for single functions, what can draw people to open-minded spaces? What combination of functions creates viable public space?

Second, an economic challenge. As we have learned, a civic square that excludes commerce itself becomes a kind of single-minded space. A vital public space needs an economic base, but how can this base be sustained in places that are already failing economically?

Third, a design challenge. How can physical design changes achieve civic and economic objectives in a context where older models no longer apply? The old mall formula was a remarkable and unexpected synthesis of disparate elements, some drawn from traditional urbanism going back to the Greek agora and others from commercial and even industrial design. The question for older shopping centers is whether they can be rethought and reconfigured in a new way to create open-minded space.

Addressing Redress

David Smiley
Columbia University

The meanings implied in the term *redress* range from remedy to repair, from reparation to compensation. That such a term could be applied to the troubled inner suburban shopping centers that are the subject of this book requires an understanding of the mall as an integral feature of the ever-expanding urban and suburban landscape and an appreciation of the social life of the millions of Americans who feel quite at home in the shopping center. The work collected for this book embraces the pivotal role played by the shopping center and is based on a conviction that failing centers can once again become integral parts of their communities.

In the decades after World War II, many urbanites left their apartments and small homes to settle at the periphery of older, high-density cities such as New York or in newer, low-density cities like Los Angeles. While this phenomenon had been underway since the 19th century, the postwar scale and intensity of suburban residential growth were unprecedented. Following close behind this residential expansion was a relatively new form of retailing organization called the shopping center (the term "mall" did not come into use until the 1960s), which provided suburbanites with easy access to downtown department stores, specialty stores, and local services. These shopping centers were portrayed by their owners, designers, and many of their users, with varying degrees of sincerity, as new community gathering places as much as retailing facilities. Famed

Cross County Shopping Center, Bronx, NY, 1955; Lathrop Douglass, architect. An early model of the "planned regional shopping center" in which small stores, a large anchor store, and a small office building were organized around landscaped, outdoor, green spaces.

mall architect Victor Gruen, perhaps lifting a term from the architectural theorist Sigfried Giedion, called the shopping center a "crystallization point" in the vast residential expanses of the emerging suburban landscape. Advocates like Gruen believed that the new shopping centers would give order and shape to mushrooming suburbs, and he predicted that greater social interaction and richer public life would be created in these new environments.

Postwar shopping centers did indeed become the focus of social life for many Americans, but in the decades-long process of suburban expansion, not all shopping centers have fared well. Many shopping centers of the 1960s, 1970s, and 1980s were remarkably successful, but they increasingly became victims of their own success as the waves of development they once led inexorably passed them by. Bigger and more lucrative shopping malls built on cheaper, undeveloped land further from denser, urban areas transformed into sad shells the proud icons of an earlier wave of suburbanization. As noted by many of the contributors to *Redressing the Mall*, a substantial percentage of shopping centers have become architecturally, economically, and socially obsolete. Abandoned, boarded up, or still in their death throes, these malls no longer generate profits, no longer serve their communities, and worse, drain the financial base and social spirit from their neighborhoods. Such inner-ring shopping centers are in dire need of care and attention.

But failed shopping centers are not just a matter of deteriorating buildings and cracked parking lots. The communities in which they sit have also changed. In the past half-century, as middle-class whites moved up the real estate ladder into newer, more exurban residential developments, inner suburban communities often moved down the same ladder. This was not without benefits, since the smaller houses of older communities became affordable for less affluent and often marginalized groups aspiring to single-family homes with backyards and barbecues. Unfortunately, the older shopping centers and the business models through which they were built proved far less adaptable. Once bustling places of gathering, part-time employment, and commerce, they have become community liabilities. According to conventional wisdom, the racial, ethnic, and class portraits of the communities that now surround many older malls cannot sustain the profits and cash flow to maintain viable businesses. But conventional wisdom can be a brittle form of knowledge, and in the case of the older shopping center, such thinking fails to acknowledge that population and census studies of inner suburban communities show bustling neighborhoods filled with people who are employed, who own their homes, and are more than ready to shop and use these places for a variety of activities. Such places may not always fit into established marketing niches, but today the population density of inner suburban areas points to a high percentage of potential customers for a smarter kind of retailer, developer, banker, or designer.

This new diverse demography suggests that analyses of the mall need to transcend questions of commerce to address how these places support the public life of their communities. Redress, in this case, refers to a change in the way shopping centers are expected to function and whom they are intended to serve; in other words, redress quite literally suggests that we ask how shopping centers appear to their users. Many of the contributors to *Redressing the Mall* define the public users of shopping centers in different ways, but common concerns emerge in a consideration of the underutilized or outmoded center. Can noncommercial activities be nurtured complementary to, or even independent of, the retail activity that surrounds them? Can the older shopping center—from finance to design—be reconceived for a new, more complex, more community-serving set of uses? New malls across the country have turned to entertainment to invigorate their shopping environments, but are there other forms of public interaction that can operate in smaller, older malls? There are no uniform answers to these questions, and the texts and projects in this book broadly interpret the ways in which shopping and commercial life have affected, and been affected by, conceptions of public use, access, and regulation. At the very least, the collected work in this book creates a new set of ways to perceive and envision the shopping center.

Ultimately, however, an understanding of the use of public space in older shopping centers (as in many redevelopment projects) often amounts to a discussion of what constitutes public space and, more precisely, who will foot the bill for its creation and maintenance. Some observers decry the treatment of public space as a mere amenity or a mere backdrop for shopping. The shopping center is, of course, an economic entity as much as a physical one, but if public space is treated solely as icing on the cake in shopping environments, we run the risk of eliding or homogenizing the diversity such space presumes to foster. In contrast, other observers have pointed out that stores, market places, plazas, parks, and even streets have historically been highly accommodating to unanticipated and alternative uses. According to this position, regulated and programmed uses at best provide an appearance of control while, in practice, different groups and individuals find ways to make the space their own. Across this range of possible uses, there are always owners and institutions with legally sanctioned and obvious control, but when the shopping environment is as close to public space as most citizens ever get, advocates of different stripes must at least recognize the necessity for a certain elasticity in interpretations of the term "public." Thus, the work in this book does not reject commercial uses of space, nor do the projects and authors reject the interaction of public money with private money in the implementation of redevelopment projects. Whether through compromise, *Realpolitik*, or calculation, the design, financial, and planning communities involved with the underutilized shopping center recognize that its problems are too complex—and the layers of ownership, history, and social change too thick—to enable a clear-cut rendering of what is and is not public. In this ambiguity, there is great potential.

What remains important is that all contributors to *Redressing the Mall* understand that there are a variety of ways in which the older shopping center can be reconfigured to embrace new uses and communities. In that spirit, the book joins voices and interests that have not historically shared the same space. Architects, developers, planners, cultural officials, builders, bankers, and historians have come together to find new ways to address each other and to examine possibilities for the ailing inner suburban shopping center.

The first part of the book, "The Shopping Mall in Context," examines the historical formation and contemporary operation of shopping centers and how these places have been altered by social, economic, demographic, legal, and political processes. Implicit, when not explicit, in these discussions is the deep interconnection and tension between the mall as a place of commerce and the mall as a community node. This sets the stage for the second part of the book, "Case Studies," which examines the current condition of several very different inner suburban shopping centers. In various states of decay and redevelopment, all are desperately in need of intervention and improvement. These studies demonstrate that the decline of older shopping centers is intimately tied to local historical, geographical, economic, and political dynamics. The studies also affirm that there are no simple or abstract formulas through which redevelopment should always take place.

"Redevelopment: Projects, Strategies, Research," the third part of the book, highlights design methods through which shopping centers and other public spaces have been configured and reconfigured. This section offers a variety of design projects to show how built additions, insertions, building types, open spaces, and programs have been combined to create new public uses. Not all the featured projects are for shopping centers, but all demonstrate design methods that could be applicable to rethinking and reusing the shopping center as a new public place. They demonstrate a remarkable range of architectural, planning, and landscape possibilities through which the older shopping center might be rethought. Integral to these strategies are the design competitions, planning and design studios, and design guidelines discussed at the end of this section. These often speculative forums can broaden the intellectual, design, and social arena in which the discussion of shopping centers takes place, and they help reframe the shopping center as part of a larger set of design and community issues. The concluding portion of the book, "Development Issues and Problems," is a realistic and sobering appraisal of the economics of shopping center reuse for which designers, architects, political officials, and public agencies must be responsible if they are to redress the ailing shopping center.

But failed shopping centers are not just
a matter of deteriorating buildings and
cracked parking lots. The communities
in which they sit have also changed.

—David Smiley

I

The Shopping Mall in Context: History and Politics

In this section, three noted scholars examine the historical, institutional, and legal frameworks that have shaped the shopping mall and raise questions about the present and future role of the shopping center in American society.

Suburban Life and Public Space

Margaret Crawford
Harvard University

Three dominant narratives have shaped the history of the American shopping mall. The first depicts the mall as a building type based on a rigid and highly inflexible format, largely determined by real estate economies, marketing research, and architectural behaviorism. The outcome of this story is the generic suburban regional mall, reproduced from coast to coast. The second narrative portrays the mall as a fundamentally anti-urban force, fostering the growth of what is commonly known as sprawl, defined as the antithesis of livable urban space and incapable of providing genuine urban experience. The third narrative sees the mall as a vehicle for a continuous process of commodification, through which a wide range of social and communal experiences and public spaces are swallowed up by commerce.

In order to broaden the picture of the mall, I would like to "deconstruct" these narratives—to question some of the assumptions on which they are based and to provide counter-examples that show that malls operate in ways distinctly different from the views offered by the usual narratives.

If we look at the history of suburban shopping malls, we find that these three views are not only misdirected but that they preclude a deeper understanding of how we might address the necessity of change. First, rather than acting as single, rigid forms, malls have been amazingly

The enclosed mall created a focused atrium space, a zone of urban intensity.

adaptable building types. They have continuously adjusted, reinvented, and retooled themselves in response to multiple economic and social changes; they take many forms and have flourished in a variety of settings. Second, malls have functioned not as agents of urban disorder but as agents of planning and order. This is especially the case in the amorphous suburbs that proliferated after World War II, where the mall provided a community focus and a centralizing element. As a result, many observers saw malls as a positive force in shaping suburban life. Finally, I want to suggest that in the long run, the processes that critics have seen as generating the malls' debilitating social effects are more complex than they imagine. We need to see commerce and commodification not as inevitable, one-directional controlling processes but as a complex condition that can be partial, temporal, and even reversible, creating situations of decommodification.

In any study of shopping malls, the concept of "public space" also needs to be scrutinized. Public space should be viewed not as a single, unified physical and social entity but as a situation that can be experienced in multiple, partial, and even paradoxical ways. Thus, there is no single public space but as many different public spaces as there are different publics. All of this suggests that the complex process of malling can be directed in a variety of directions by changing any one or combination of such elements as public policy, regulation, financing, ownership, and management, as well as physical form and design.

The earliest places that we recognize as shopping centers date from the 1920s and 1930s. Among the innovations of the time was the organization of these new centers under a single owner and manager. Country Club Plaza, developed by Jesse Clyde Nichols in Kansas City in 1922, is the most famous. Designed as part of a larger suburban subdivision, it was intended to be an alternative town center or miniature downtown for the new residents. The physical organization of the project was based on the urban block, with separate buildings housing shops and offices but designed in a single, coherent manner. This was also among the earliest instances in which a private developer rather than a public entity provided civic amenities such as fountains, benches, small parks, public art, and public services. Highland Park, Dallas, of 1931, was similar to Country Club Plaza and followed the urban block mode. Places such as these were considered to be community centers, and their owners often sponsored Christmas celebrations, art fairs, and dog shows. They remained, however, commercial ventures, intended to make money and reinforce elite images of upscale suburban life.

During the 1930s and 1940s, planners and urbanists—especially those connected to the Regional Plan Association of America (RPAA)—utilized the shopping center as a fundamental element in their strategies for decentralization. In planned towns like Greenbelt, Maryland (1936), designers placed the shopping center at the center of the community's social life, building on the earlier work of Clarence Stein and Henry Wright. Mixing the commercial services necessary for a new development with civic and recreational spaces, these designers and planners argued for a new type of small-town life. Critics including Lewis Mumford portrayed these communities as examples of a new settlement pattern that could serve as an alternative to both the sprawl and disorder of the suburban strip and the increasingly frantic overcrowding of urban downtowns.

These developments, however, occurred at a small scale. The major explosion of shopping centers came after World War II when the familiar model of the "dumbbell" mall (department store "anchors" connected by an outdoor pedestrian mall) appeared. Among the earliest of the type was Shoppers World in Framingham, Massachusetts, which opened with great fanfare in October 1951. These new malls were created out of necessity to provide shopping and services for new and quickly growing suburban areas. The centers typically included both large department stores and such everyday services as supermarkets, drug stores, and dry cleaners. The safe and protected pedestrian malls and courts also housed tot lots, chapels, community rooms, and a host of temporary activities including art exhibits, dances, and fashion shows. These activities, typically addressed to women and children, continued the suburban tradition of domesticated public space. The low-key design of the open-air malls, decorated with public art and landscaping, also mirrored the image of suburban housing design.

At the time, architects, planners, and developers saw the new shopping centers as a way to reform the fragmented nature of development in both urban and suburban areas. The centers provided an important centrality and focus for dispersed suburban settlements. In effect, the new centers offered what many observers considered to be "better" planned downtowns with easy parking and convenient one-stop shopping.

The primary theorist of this type of shopping mall was Victor Gruen. An architect rather than a developer, Gruen attempted to redesign the suburban mall to recreate the complexity and vitality of urban experience without the noise, dirt, and confusion that had come to characterize popular images of the city. Gruen identified shopping as part of a larger web of human activities, arguing that merchandising would be more successful if commercial activities were integrated with cultural enrichment and relaxation. He saw mall design as a way of producing new town centers or what he called "shopping towns." Thus he encouraged mall developers to include in their plans as many nonretail functions as possible, adding cultural, artistic, and social events. He called this integration of commerce with community life "environmental architecture."

At a larger scale, Gruen saw the mall principally as an urban ordering device that, if used rationally, could replace the messy and illogical form of the American city with harmonious and sociable urban patterns. In 1955, he proposed to transform the entire downtown of Fort Worth, Texas, visually and spatially by applying the lessons of the suburban shopping center. His plan improved traffic circulation, separated pedestrian and automobile traffic, and integrated commercial and noncommercial activities by organizing them around multiple plazas and squares. Most importantly, he provided 60,000 parking places, making the center easily accessible.

Gruen also built the next breakthrough in mall design—the enclosed mall—at Southdale, outside Minneapolis, in 1956. The enclosed mall created a focused atrium space, a zone of urban intensity, energized by plunging elevators and zigzagging escalators. It dramatically reshaped the retail mix by expelling convenient everyday shopping to the strip in

Aerial view of a typical
1960s enclosed mall.

favor of stores featuring clothing, gifts, and impulse items. At the same time, its covered, climate-controlled spaces (especially in places like Minnesota) suggested new forms of public and civic life. Drawing huge crowds to performances of the Minneapolis Symphony, annual balls, high school proms, restaurants and cafes, and dozens of social events, Southdale vastly expanded the role of the mall as social and community center.

Over the next two decades, as the enclosed mall expanded into regional, super-regional, and megamall sizes, it generated its own activities and forms of social life. Girl scouts camped in malls; singles met in seemingly benign surroundings; mothers and infants, as well as older people, gathered in cold weather; and on hot days, almost everyone went to the mall. Malls also became important work places, providing women and teenagers with convenient, if low-paid, jobs. The mall even created such now-familiar social types as mall walkers, mall rats, and valley girls. Finally, malls became magnets for concentrated suburban development activity, serving as important regional nodes attracting adjacent uses such as hotels, offices, and other urban forms. Providing concentrated communal and commercial activities, the mall served as the heart of what are known today as "edge cities."

By the end of the 1970s, regional and super-regional malls had saturated the market and covered the American landscape in patterns that mirrored an area's buying power. Successful older malls were renovated and enclosed to maintain their market share, but the continued success of generic or older mall types was no longer assured. New and more complex forms of production and consumption fragmented income, employment, and spending patterns into a more complex mosaic. This led to a multiplication and diversification of retailing and mall types into a broader range of more specialized and flexible forms, which allowed for a more precise match between goods and consumers.

Such specialization occurred across a wide economic and programmatic spectrum. The earliest new form was the festival marketplace pioneered by James Rouse. Rouse took malls from the suburbs to historic or scenic urban locations as part of a larger strategy of urban revitalization in places such as the restored Faneuil Hall in Boston, of 1976. He reconfigured the merchandising mix to feature food and souvenir shops alongside noncommercial tourist venues such as museums and historic ships. Most importantly, Rouse blurred the boundaries between the mall and the urban setting.

Another new niche was the specialty mall, which dispensed with existing formulas such as the department store anchor to focus on specific markets, locations, and goods. This type included luxury malls, often using historic or European themes, such as 2 Rodeo in Beverly Hills or the Borgata in Scottsdale, Arizona. At the other end of the spectrum was the outlet mall whose large size and minimal design communicated discount and bargain shopping. Most recently, the entertainment mall has changed the mall environment with a mix devoted to movies, recreational activities, nightclubs, and restaurants, with limited but specialized shopping. These malls are often developed by media corporations: City Walk, in Los Angeles, is run by Universal Studios; San Francisco's Metreon, by Sony. Most widespread, however, has been the rebirth of the small roadside shopping center, the mini-mall. In Los Angeles, more than 5000 mini-malls have appeared over the past decade, and similar development has flourished in many other large urban areas. Although usually

Faneuil Hall,
Boston, Massachusetts.

Borgata,
Scottsdale, Arizona.

specializing in convenience and quick service, the mini-malls reflect their neighborhood settings, often utilizing a broad range of ethnic styles and merchandise.

Several trends can be discerned from this trajectory that lend themselves to the subject of the reuse of shopping malls and the question of public space.

Contesting "Publicness"

The definition of the "publicness" of the mall is not a simple given nor is it irrevocably structured by ownership, management, or court rulings. It is can always be struggled over and even renegotiated. This can occur in even the most rigidly programmed setting, such as the enormous Mall of America built in 1995. The Mall of America, connected by public transportation to downtown Minneapolis, was often crowded by thousands of minority teenagers, or what the management called "inner-city youth," who were using it as a gathering space on weekend nights. Mall management attempted to find ways to demonstrate the nonpublicness of the place, such as forbidding access to anyone without adult supervision or hiring security guards. After much discussion, influenced by the minority community—which was outraged by the situation—mall management made a former Macy's basement (which wasn't working as retail space) available as a youth club, supervised by students from the mall's continuing education high school. This tacit acknowledgment of "the public's" right to at least some of the mall's space undermines the purely commercial logic of the mall.

Stealth Malls

Malls sometimes succeed by submerging or hiding their stereotypical features. In Pasadena, California, a new mall called One Colorado is so seamlessly integrated into the conventional urban blocks and street fronts of its neighborhood that, except for small plaques announcing that it is actually private property, it is not recognizable as a mall. The mall operates as the lynchpin of the consolidated redevelopment and revitalization of "Old Town Pasadena." In this case, the mall, rather than the city, pro-

One Colorado,
Pasadena, California.

vides an open plaza that is widely used as a pedestrian walkway and gathering place. Other developers, rather than starting from scratch, are building in and around existing buildings and businesses. The Beverly Connection, in Los Angeles, combines a varied mix of everyday retailers including supermarkets, drug stores, coffee shops, and restaurants with entertainment and retail uses in adjacent buildings. Acting as a link between a several block area of malls and mini-malls, it consolidates them into a dense and crowded urban cluster. This blurs the boundaries between public and private in ways that deserve more attention.

De- and Re- Malling

"Dead" or unsuccessful malls can be radically reconfigured physically, architecturally, and programmatically. A well-known icon of mall culture, the Sherman Oaks Galleria in Los Angeles, has been turned into an office building with a food court. In an ongoing project, architects and planners are performing radical surgery on Plaza Pasadena, a typical 1980s urban enclosed mall shopping. By removing the mall's large central section, they reconnected it the to the city's street grid, reinstating a logical connection to the town's beaux-arts civic center. The remaining parts of the mall will also be reconfigured to contain small shops and offices with 400 apartments above.

With experts now estimating the average mall life at less than 10 years, enclosed malls are undergoing complete transformation and redefinition. They are removing their roofing, dismantling relentless corridors, and punching through windowless walls to let in light and air. They are changing every aspect of conventional mall wisdom. In many ways, however, this is just a more dramatic version of the continual updating and evolution that have always characterized mall development.

New Mall Types

Altered financial, social, and political circumstances continue to produce new types of malls. In Canada, Chinese immigrants, responding to Canadian government investment requirements for immigration, have reorganized the structure and financing of malls to create more hybrid typologies. In the Richmond suburb of Vancouver, several malls juxtapose mini-mall shops opening onto surface parking with more conventional multistory enclosed malls with rooftop parking. Instead of having a single owner, mall shops are sold to individual owners under a "strata" form of ownership similar to that of condominiums. This allows owners to subdivide and lease their spaces. In addition, spaces in the mall's aisles and atrium are rented out for booths, tables, and even rugs.

Without centralized control, these spaces have a dense, bazaar-like quality defined by extreme juxtapositions of size, décor, and use. There is a wild mix of retailing with everything from clothing and food to insurance and car accessories, all of which are highly responsive to changing local tastes and needs. The mall also hosts many local events, specializing in children's performances and Chinese holidays. Nearby, a more controlled but still hybrid mall stacks two floors of shops with two floors of offices and a top floor occupied by a large Buddhist temple and monastery.

This brings us full circle: malls have now become so diverse that they are virtually synonymous with retailing. Americans now shop in malls that look like cities and in cities that look like malls. Given the extraordinary flexibility of this form of commercial development, it is difficult to predict the future directions the mall might take. But, if we can learn from the mall's past, we will be more likely to be able to shape its future.

Civic Space

Benjamin R. Barber
Walt Whitman Center for the Culture and Politics of Democracy,
Rutgers University

The mall has come to embody many of the dilemmas of a privatized
and commercialized society that compels every institution to pay its own
way as measured by monies earned and quarterly profits distributed.[1]
Although in practice the mall has achieved some of the variety and plural-
ism typical of all American institutions as they spread into distinctive
regions and subcultures, I will focus on an ideal (if hardly ideal!)
paradigm. Certainly, there are malls that offer relatively diverse fare,
are not dominated by "big boxes," try to integrate restaurants and other
more leisurely venues into their commercial space, and are accessible to
public transportation. (Many of these exist in the vicinity of university
campuses.) But the dominant model is a big box anchored enclosed space
dominated by boutiques and specialty stores catering almost exclusively to
shoppers and without significant public transportation access. Malls of
this kind define the genre: they are not only the centerless centerpieces of
suburbs (in which more than half of America now lives) but are becoming
models for urban revival as well. Ironically, at the very moment when the
city is reappearing in the suburbs under the sanitized guise of the "new
urbanism," the suburbs are invading cities through the malling of commercial neighborhoods and the displacement of seedy authenticity by
anodyne artifice.

      The mall stands as a powerful embodiment of the privatization and commercialization of space associated with the forces of what I have called MacWorld, turning our complex, multiuse public space into a one-dimensional venue for consumption. The sameness of the architecture and interior design, and of the goods and entertainment offered, no longer has the excuse Howard Johnson and the Hilton once offered the weary traveler: comforting conformity in an otherwise alien world. Sameness now is a matter of efficiency, volume, and cultural homogeneity. Even the tie-in with multiplex movie houses is about consumer conformity and the selling of films that are more and more closely tied to music, fast food, and other commodities in which the mall specializes. The multiplex is the mall's consumer academy. A film like *Titanic* that is an industry unto itself (at more than a billion dollars in revenues), puts a half-dozen books on the best-seller list, sells not only its prize-winning song but Celine Dion, music generally, and the hardware needed to play it, [and] is typical of the vertical integration of modern commodities in what I have called the "infotainment telesector."…

The pervasiveness of consumer identity today is evident in market research profiles, which classify people not by race or gender or even traditional class, but by segmented market inclinations. Clarita, a Virginia marketing firm, charts potential customers and their behavior by reference to such nouveau niche categories as "pools and patios," "shotguns and pickups," "Bohemian mix," and "urban gold coast." Identity itself is increasingly associated with branding and commercial logos. If to be branded was once the melancholy fate of cattle and slaves, today business adviser Tom Peters (in his *Brand You*) tells his customers with satisfaction, "You're every bit as much a brand as Nike, Coke, Pepsi, or the Body Shop." The first step for someone who wants to brand himself is to "write your own mission statement, to guide you as CEO of Me, Inc."[2]

This consumerist one-dimensionality achieves a palpable geography in the controlled and controlling architecture of the shopping mall. Malls are the privatized public squares of the new fringe city "privatopia," which uses secession from the larger common society—deemed vulgar, multiethnic, and dangerous—to secure a gated world of placid safety. Cut off wherever possible from public transportation (and the suspect publics it serves),[3] denuded of political and civic activities (often with the help of State Supreme Court decisions declaring the enclosed space of malls to be private and thus not subject to the rights of assembly and free expression that would apply in public space), the mall becomes the cathedral of our new secular civilization.[4] It would be too much to call the mall's consumerist culture totalitarian, freighted as that term is with the 20th century's most egregious horrors. But inasmuch as the mall replicates a one-dimensional life in which every activity other than shopping vanishes, there is certainly something totalizing about its defining activities. The mall refuses to play host to churches or synagogues, to community theaters or art galleries, to political speech or civic leafleting, to clinics, childcare centers, schools, granges, town halls, or social services of any kind.

On entering an enclosed mall, we are asked to shed every identity other than that of the consumer. Eating is about buying fast food and moving back into the stream of shoppers; entertainment means buying Hollywood's latest and all the commodities that go with it; hanging out and people-watching are discouraged by security guards and, more important, the architecture is designed to impede sitting or standing around and to keep the traffic flow moving into the shops. On weekend evenings, teens may try to behave as they once did on Main Street strips, and in the course of rainy afternoons, seniors may look to stroll and loiter as they once might have done at a town post office or corner barber shop or general store. But malls are neither designed for nor encouraged to serve such purposes.[5] Food is available in "fuel-up pit stops" but not in restaurants where shoppers might while away valuable shopping time over a social dinner. Clocks are nowhere to be seen—time stands still for the shopper who must, under no circumstances, be reminded that it may be time to be somewhere else.

Indeed, nowadays, malls do not even pretend to sell necessities. No dry cleaner's, no hardware store, no vegetable market, no laundry, no place to pick up eggs or milk or a bottle of sherry or a newspaper. Mall developers and their vendors prefer theme and specialty stores and ubiquitous boutiques like The Museum Store, Warner Bros., The Sharper

Image, Brookstone's, The Nature Store, and The Disney Store that sell you nothing you want until you get inside and realize you need everything they sell....

Overhauling the Mall

This is the challenge for those who are critics of the dominant trends in modern American architecture and planning and dissatisfied with the responses to date. Suburbanization has meant secession, sprawl, and the destruction of community. The "new urbanism" has addressed the loss of vitality in the suburbs in a primarily cosmetic way, opting for the appearance of cities but avoiding those essential urban traits such as class and race mixing, the delight real urban dwellers take in the unfamiliar, tolerance and even affinity for disorder, and the ubiquity of risk. Yet these are precisely the rough and vital substance of real cities....

If...[some critics celebrate] the meretricious anarchy of the suburbs, confirmed haters of suburbanization tend to indulge a secessionist strategy of their own, withdrawing into boutiqued cities that have practiced "urban removal" where they can feel at home and leaving suburbanites to their tawdry little destinies. Or they dream of getting people out of the suburbs and back into small towns. They wage quixotic campaigns against big box stores like Wal-Mart and the Home Depot, and yearn to close the malls so that downtowns will spring back to life—but at the expense of less economically privileged suburbanites who benefit from the low costs and multiple consumer options of the big box megastores.[6] Nostalgia for small-town America dies hard in a nation where so many people spend the first 20 years of their lives trying to escape the parochialism of the small towns where they grew up, and the remainder of their lives wishing they could somehow go home again.

I would offer a less radical and more realistic approach. If a privatizing ideology and a consumerist culture have turned citizens into consumers, we need to go to where the consumers are and try to turn them back into citizens. If they go to the net and then become passive spectators to what is supposed to be an interactive technology, we need to "reinteractivate" the net. If they go to the mall in search of public space

34

and are seduced into privatized shopping behavior, we need to confront and transform the mall. The aim is not to get people off the Internet but to get civic, cultural, and educational activity on it, not to close the malls or lure people out of them but to make them more like the multiuse public spaces they have displaced.

Given the ubiquity of malls, it makes more sense to rethink the laws, politics, zoning policies, development incentives, and architectural predilections that have forged our particular version of suburban life. Which changes might encourage the reconfiguring of commercial space in the suburbs? There is considerable latitude even within the confines of purely commercial development for variety: Big box or small store outlets? Open-space parking, parking deck, or traditional strip-mall doorfront parking? Public-transportation access or parking lots only? Integration of residential housing or purely commercial? Just shopping or subsidies for public art and traditional grocery store and dry cleaner vendors?...Cities have used tax incentives and building permit requirements to induce developers to offer public sculptures, park space, and a livable, environmentally accommodating architecture along with new retail and corporate space....The answer to these questions obviously impinges on the character of the public space a retail mall creates.

There is plenty of room for experimentation. Malls have been overbuilt in the suburbs, some estimate by 30 percent or more. This means failed malls and empty stores even in the successful ones. Meanwhile, people have tired of the monotonous unidimensionality of the mall experience, and the average visit has declined from well over to well under two hours. In short, while flourishing in many ways, malls are troubled enough to incite anxiety in developers and vendors, who are looking for new forms of collaboration with the civic and residential communities they serve. In many cases this amounts to little more than a search for a new promotion concept, a gimmick that gets people back into the stores. But what looks like a gimmick to a developer may turn out to entail a relatively serious deprivatization of retail space. A renewed civic life instigated by, say, a second-hand bookstore or a community performance stage or a life-size chess set at the heart of a mall may give new hope to retailers even as it allows customers to think of themselves as neighbors and citizens....

There are a variety of ordinary institutions that can be found in any urban neighborhood or rural town that could serve to diversify a shopping center: a school, a post office, performance stage, or a childcare center, a speakers' corner, a public library, a recreation area, or a public-access cable studio, an Internet cafe, a teen club, an art gallery, a playground, an interdenominational prayer hall. The presence of such facilities would do more than introduce variety: it would turn private back into public space, and it would lace commercial behavior with a dose of civic activity, allowing customers to reconceive themselves as neighbors and citizens as well.

There are a number of points of leverage that might move both private developers and public officials in a civic direction. The development of an appropriate civic architecture that takes the mall as its starting place would offer realistic designs to committed developers. Public officials can utilize zoning laws, permits for curb cuts that allow developers access from the highway, and environmental and safety regulations as both carrots and sticks to modify developers' behavior. The courts can be used to argue the case that malls are public rather than private and must allow public and political activity. Currently, about a dozen states have taken a legal position or, like New Hampshire, are hearing cases, with New Jersey, California, and Colorado having ruled that free-speech rights are protected in enclosed malls, implying that they enclose public rather than private space. Finally, public transportation and road patterns can do much to determine whether malls become suburban neighborhoods or isolated, upscale retail megaplazas unrelated to their surrounding ecological and demographic territories.

Antidotes to Sprawl

Kevin Mattson
Contemporary History Institute and Department of History,
Ohio University

The regional shopping center faces a crisis today; some even speculate that it might die. Therefore, it is important to recognize that there are bottom-line economic reasons for developers to listen to those who want to make the mall into something more than a conduit for consumerism. Can the American shopping mall become a mixed-use space where citizens gather for political and cultural events in addition to shopping? Can the mall be a place where public art and intriguing civic design are put to energetic use?

The Mall as a Zone of Private Consumption

The shopping mall was an integral part of the post–World War II suburbanization in America. It symbolized the ideals of consumerism and economic abundance that drew many Americans to the suburbs. But one of its original proponents, Victor Gruen, believed the shopping mall could serve as a "crystallization point for suburbia's community life" and become an *antidote* to suburban sprawl, not a contributor.[1]

Some designers of malls still speak the language of community and place today. For instance, a recent proposal in Silver Spring, Maryland, for a large mall to be called "American Dream" was billed by its developers as a "town center for Silver Spring".[2] Nonetheless, most mall designers and developers reject this line of reasoning. For them, the mall has one function and one function alone—to encourage shopping. The spokesperson for a mall outside of Providence, Rhode Island, was recently quoted as saying: "Some of the elements that went into the mall were specifically designed to make it less accommodating. People question why there aren't outdoor park benches or aren't planters at heights where people can sit, and the reason is because you don't want to encourage people to just come and hang out. You want them to come in and use it for the purpose it was designed for—to shop, be entertained, and dine. The mall is reserved for use of mall patrons, and if you're not a mall patron, you'll be asked to move along."[3] This is a quintessential statement on the mall as a private zone for consumption—a vision that has dominated the design of malls ever since architects like Gruen became successful.

The purpose of the mall as a one-dimensional environment for shopping is highlighted when citizens try to use malls for something else. Realizing that malls are places to connect with fellow citizens, some have decided to treat them as public spaces. The activities of citizens who leaflet, protest, or otherwise use malls as public space have resulted in a number of contentious court cases—all of which have forced mall owners to spell out their argument that the mall is a purely private space and prompted important debate about the privatization of space. Early federal rulings, from the United States Supreme Court led by Earl Warren in the late 1960s, favored the free speech rights of citizens over the private property rights of the shopping center owners. But in the 1970s, the Court—then led by Warren Berger—changed its position and ruled in successive cases that certain free speech acts did infringe on shopping center owners' property rights without significantly enhancing free speech. The federal Court shifted this recurring legal debate to the state level in a 1980 ruling (*PruneYard Shopping Center vs. Robbins*), which said that any state could extend its free speech protections beyond the federal standards. Since then, many state rulings have been in favor of property rights, but some states—including California, Oregon, Massachusetts, Colorado, Washington, and New Jersey—have ruled in favor of more extensive free speech activities and validated the concept of malls as public spaces.[4]

These legal rulings have addressed the current dilemma of public space and suburban shopping centers. Arguments made in favor of the free speech rights of citizens often claim that speech is not really free unless it is allowed to reach the public. Since the public goes to malls, the reasoning goes, free speech and other political or civic activity must be allowed there. For instance, in 1968 when Thurgood Marshall argued that a shopping center in Pennsylvania had to abide by the First Amendment protections, he argued that malls were the "functional equivalent" of a downtown in pre-automobile cities. More recently, in a ruling in Colorado, the state supreme court argued that a mall "functioned as a latter-day public forum" and needed to recognize this de facto role and allow protesters.[5] This "public forum" principle is often at the center of current state court debates. The central idea is that people need spaces in which they can conceive of themselves as citizens committed to political debate and persuasion and as neighbors with common educational and cultural needs.

The tension between malls as public spaces and malls as private property has also been addressed in legal debates about the public funding or incentives provided to mall developers. Free speech advocates believe that since cities and local governments help to support malls in a number of ways (i.e., taxation incentives and development grants), malls are not only private but also, by necessity, public. In a recent district court decision in favor of the rights of anti-fur activists who protested in the largest mall in the U.S., the Mall of America in Minnesota, the judge agreed with this view bluntly, writing "a publicly funded private entity is a contradiction in terms."[6] But mall managers and others arguing for the primacy of private property rights have rejected this view as a misunderstanding of the shopping center's relation to the local community and the public. In the Minnesota case (which mall managers eventually won), a Mall of America manager refuted the judge's position on the grounds that the public money provided for the mall was "for the sole purpose of stimulating economic development" and that the profitable Mall has more than repaid the money through tourism revenues. This echoes other mall managers and owners who argue that the sole purpose of the mall is shopping and that assuring the safety and comfort of shoppers requires management to control any activities that might disturb them.[7] What these court cases make clear is that mall owners want shopping malls to remain dedicated to one purpose only—the safe facilitation of private consumption.

Cracks in the Modern Shopping Center

A certain irony has emerged in recent years. While shopping center owners have argued that their sole responsibility is to facilitate consumption, new forms of shopping have started to challenge the mall. In comparison to a suburban shopper in the 1950s, a current shopper has more "places" to buy things, many of which offer quicker access to "overworked" suburbanites.[8] Key here are big box stores (Wal-Mart, etc.) that offer shoppers all items under one roof; catalog shopping that allows people to purchase goods without leaving their homes; and more recently "e-commerce" and on-line shopping sites. These new forms of consumption consistently portray themselves as alternatives to shopping at malls....[9]

Though it is too soon to say whether these new modes of shopping will do away with the shopping mall, one thing is for certain. Visitation to shopping centers has declined, many traditional anchor department stores (i.e., Caldor, Service Merchandise, etc.) have gone bankrupt and a New York City real estate firm reported that from 1997 to 1999, the average mall visit declined from one and a half hours to 40 minutes.[10] Even the industry spokesgroup—the International Council of Shopping Centers (ICSC)—admits that shopping is up on-line but down at the malls.[11]

The result of these trends is most evocatively captured in the rise of "ghost malls"—malls that have failed but are left standing. Perhaps the most emblematic symbol of these trends is represented in a recent mall failure. Sherman Oaks Galleria, a Los Angeles mall that epitomized shopping mall culture (and was featured in the movies *Valley Girl* and *Fast Times at Ridgemont High*), has recently been emptied of stores and redone as an office-retail complex.[12] Michael Beyard, of the Urban Land Institute, recently predicted that 15 to 20 percent of the 2,200 enclosed shopping malls around the country will be obliged to close in the near future.[13]

Some mall owners have responded by creating simplistic marketing attempts to build loyalty. They have offered "awards" to shoppers, like prepaid phone cards, magazine subscriptions, and other free items.[14] Others have suggested fighting mall vacancies by...merely attracting newer, more lucrative forms of retail.[15] But there also seems a general recognition that the shopping mall needs to offer people something more.

Making Malls Something More

Recently, leading developers have recognized the decline in shopping center retail and have begun to experiment with ways to draw the public back to the mall by delving into new forms of civic design and public space. Despite significant differences, all these innovations involve diversifying and "complexifying" what has become an overly simplistic design and retailing formula.

An important diversifying initiative has been the Sony Corporation's Metreon in San Francisco, developed for Sony by Millennium Partners with architect Gary Handel.[16] Metreon is an "urban entertainment destination," which brings together shopping, eating, and entertainment. Its design draws not only from the enclosed shopping center but from the theme park, from the urban festival marketplace pioneered by James Rouse at Boston's Faneuil Hall, and from the traditional urban street. The Metreon combines a dozen movie theaters, an Imax theater, one-of-a-kind stores, and restaurants which replace traditional mall anchors and shops. While projects like Sony's Metreon have been emulated by competitors such as Disney and Dreamworks, the scale of the project makes it a very expensive investment that requires a booming downtown with ample tourist traffic. Could the Metreon concept be repackaged in a form that would be applicable to the inner-ring suburb? Moreover, could such success in diversifying the mall be extended to include genuine civic space?

In fact, there are numerous developers who have responded to citizens' desires to make malls into community centers. The ICSC has documented the inclusion of public libraries, chapels, community health centers, and other public-minded institutions in malls.[17] In his 1995 *City Life*, Witold Rybczynski describes how the DeBartolo Corporation and the Rouse Company have encouraged community activities in their malls. Another initiative in this vein was the "Town Hall in the Mall" project in Everett, Washington. An outreach center for City Hall in a shopping mall, this experiment showed clear signs of civic success—for example, by registering more people to vote than the City Hall downtown.[18] An increasing number of malls, including the huge Mall of America in Minnesota, also contain educational facilities such as space for community college courses and high school equivalency test training.

It should be recognized that these are random experiments, most with little overall civic vision, done out of an immediate desire to fill vacant stores. Many of the public functions such as libraries were not even incorporated into the mall. They were ghettoized, tucked away in some obscure corner where few shoppers would find them. Only the exceptional work of a few innovators has really shown just what can be done to address mall fatigue while also enhancing civic life.

Civic Innovators

A few developers have tried to incorporate more civic and community space into shopping malls. In the 1980s, Ron Sher, developer of the Mall at the Crossroads in Bellevue, Washington (outside of Seattle), purchased a mall that had become a center of crime and drug dealing—a typical example of a failing, inner-ring shopping center.[19] The surrounding neighborhood was dense and diverse but lacked any real downtown. Sher believed the center could be revitalized if it adapted to the community. Since there was already an upscale mall close by, which drew many high-income shoppers, Sher put in a mix of stores (including a grocery store) that could be of use to local residents and encouraged community life. Among its many activities, the mall sponsored live entertainment on weekends, community candidate forums, and a children's reading club. Sher revitalized the mall by making it something more than a mere shopping center.[20]

Doug Storrs' development of Mashpee Commons on Cape Cod provides another example of civic innovation. Storrs acquired a well located but run-down strip mall and revitalized it by using the New England town as a model. Storrs transformed the strip mall into a new development that included stores, offices, residential space, and a centrally located post office (which draws in pedestrians). In addition, a library, church, school, police station and public squares are incorporated into the overall plan. Storrs also planned the mall so that pedestrians from a newly designed adjacent neighborhood could add to the mix of functions and public spaces. Following the principles of higher density and mixed use, Storrs literally built the mall into a new community.[21]

One of the most exciting retail transformations is taking place at Willingboro Plaza in Willingboro, New Jersey. Originally built by William Levitt during the 1950s, the town is today a predominantly African American community, and its commercial corridor is marked by dead strip malls. Although Willingboro Plaza backs directly onto the town, it has become a "ghost mall" with 13 shuttered buildings on 56 acres.[22] Recently, representatives from the state and local government, architects, and Robert Stang, a civic-minded developer, have taken on the responsibility to make Willingboro Plaza into a town center. The principal planner from the Burlington County Office of Land-Use and Planning, Mark Remsa, developed an elaborate process of community input and consensus building. Two architects, Bice Wilson of Meridian Design and Randy Croxton of Croxton Collaborative Architects, drew up

New Seabury Shopping Center, c. 1965, eventual site of Mashpee Commons.

Mashpee Commons in
the 1990s.

Willingboro Plaza
existing condition.

plans based on the community meetings. Realizing that no big box stores would locate at the Plaza, they concentrated on a mix of uses including smaller retail, light industry, and—most importantly within this context— civic and public space, including a library and a community college.[23]

Many other older malls around the country are being repositioned and connected to their communities but, of course, skeptics will argue that these exceptional examples are simply that—exceptions. And certainly there is reason to believe that the industry as a whole will continue creating more ill-fated malls. Nonetheless, the broad trends look good. An April 1999 survey of large malls under construction finds that fewer than half of the 150 or so projects are single-use enclosed shopping centers surrounded by parking lots. Some malls are designed around open-air "town centers," with the parking carefully sited behind or beneath the major buildings, and about a third of the projects include mixed uses such as housing, libraries, and office space.[24]

Conclusion

In the end, the most persuasive argument for civic design rests on its own merits. As a democratic society, we need places where citizens can congregate and associate with one another. Public space is a prerequisite for a healthy civil society.[25] But this sort of argument often sounds abstract in the world of real estate and development. That is why it is important to recognize that there are reasons to believe that more mall developers will listen to arguments that malls must become multidimensional places, rather than one-dimensional conduits for shopping. Developers are starting to learn that people are not just consumers but also citizens. That is what makes the issue of the civic redesign of shopping centers so pertinent today.

The sameness of the architecture and interior design, and of the goods and entertainment offered, no longer has the excuse Howard Johnson and the Hilton once offered the weary traveler: comforting conformity in an otherwise alien world. Sameness now is a matter of efficiency, volume, and cultural homogeneity.

—Benjamin R. Barber

II

Case Studies

Few cities, towns, or suburbs have escaped the debilitating effects of underused or vacant shopping centers. The case studies that follow offer stories about some of the many places in which citizens, government officials, developers, and design and planning professionals have sought to improve an older shopping center. These stories show the complex relationships among the wide variety of participants in the redevelopment process and demonstrate the rewards and difficulties of repositioning older centers.

Repositioning the Older Shopping Mall

Marilyn Jordan Taylor Skidmore, Owings & Merrill

In a midsize city in the middle of America sit two regional malls so close to each other that they compete for the trips and dollars of the regional population. As a result both are suffering. A developer decided to buy and redevelop both malls, differentiating them in one way or another in search of an unlikely win-win solution. For the first mall, he proposes to double the number of anchors by raiding from the second mall. This strategy follows a tried and true, if sometimes short-sighted, market dictum, "grow to survive." It also creates an interesting problem for the second mall: how will its image, use, and organization diverge from the first? Among the interventions our firm has proposed are selective demolition, the introduction of a grid of streets (at approximately 300-foot centers), and the preservation of some of the anchors. Cutting the mall into pieces introduces new space for a civic plaza at the core of the project and secondary plazas sprinkled elsewhere on the site. New retail spaces, offices, theaters, restaurants, and even residential uses provide infill throughout the project and reinforce the definition of the new streets. In terms of development and finance, cutting up the older mall creates parcels of various sizes, which offer new opportunities for multiple developers, builders, and even owners. The new project, now a dense

arrangement of buildings, spaces, and uses, also offers room for landscaping, sidewalks, and on-street parking. Creating a new community and joining with existing communities around it, this transformed mall has the complex array of uses, scales, and accessibility to provide for long-term viability.

From this and other projects done by SOM, I would like to suggest four strategies that utilize existing buildings and infrastructure to reposition and revitalize older shopping centers in inner suburban areas. The first strategy is "externalizing." Retail is perhaps the most volatile land use for which we design today. The rate of change is increasing, life cycles are shrinking, and electronic retailing is a hovering cloud. In this retailing environment aging malls must adapt. For architects and urban designers this creates a great opportunity to recapture large, isolated shopping center land holdings and reintegrate them back into the settlement fabric that has grown up around them in recent decades. To do this we must break down the massive scale of the mall and its infrastructure and shift its orientation out towards its setting: that is, the mall needs to be externalized. This means drawing from local grids rather than merely inserting limited access or one

Fountain Square, with neither a square nor a fountain.

49

directional roads, designing for the pedestrian instead of the automobile, and finding new ways of utilizing public transit.

The second strategy to help reposition the shopping mall is "mixing and multiplying." After five or six decades of living with malls, it is evident that their singular conceptualization is stultifying. Over time malls have grown more and more like each other, and the same national stores with the same merchandise and the same window displays are everywhere. How can we change a half-century-old pattern that is increasingly difficult to sustain? How can we create a mix? One way of achieving a lively arrangement of building and use scales in direct proximity to each other is to encourage varied parcel sizes. This would create a new landscape for the retailing package. We also need what I would call "an origination mix." For example, no development would have more than one-third national stores; ideally at least a third would be local stores, and the remaining third would be regional stores. New and old centers would benefit from a mix of owners, each of whose size and personality could add to a sense of place.

"Going green," the third revitalization strategy is less an ecological concept than the recognition that people actually like to be out of doors. Examples in warm climates abound but Broadway—New York City's (and my own) Main Street—is crowded with pedestrians, used book sellers, and sidewalk seating at virtually all times of the year. Research has shown that a growing number of creditworthy mall tenants are also willing to locate in outdoor environments. Open spaces and landscapes can become central organizing and social spaces instead of the leftovers that they have become in recent years. In fact, these spaces are often the elements around which a community sense of ownership and stewardship is formed.

Finally, the fourth strategy is adding transit. A few years ago my firm conducted a study for New Jersey Transit titled "Planning for Transit Friendly Land Use: A Primer for Communities." Its intended audience was members of the numerous citizen, voluntary, planning, and zoning boards active throughout the state. The New Jersey State Plan already encourages the reuse of underutilized areas and was a catalyst for the study. Our primer addressed land use, cars, and community-friendly transit. We provided information about how to design transit to be friendly to communities, as well as how to design communities to be friendly to transit. Transit is an incredibly varied and formative type of infrastructure. We urged this strategy partly out of antipathy to parking garages and acres of asphalt, but more importantly, because transit riders are pedestrians. For specific parts of their journeys pedestrians interact in ways that cars never can but that communities must. Not only do pedestrians shop but they create the links and conversations that form the core of communities. Our study emphasized that successful development can take place only when local communities assume a stewardship role in defining and maintaining their open spaces, their streets, and their commercial infrastructure. This is perhaps the essential element in the repositioning of older shopping malls.

Villa Italia, Lakewood, Colorado

Mark Falcone Continuum Partners

Villa Italia, artist's rendering.

Continuum Partners is currently redeveloping Lakewood Center, a midsize mall of about 1.4 million square feet built (on 100 acres) in 1965 in the city of Lakewood, outside of Denver. Lakewood's 13 private subdivisions incorporated in 1969 to avoid being absorbed by the City of Denver, then under a busing order. The new city had no real cohesion or unity, the housing stock was weak, and the residential tax base was insufficient to properly provide services. At its peak in the 1970s, the Lakewood shopping center provided as much as 50 percent of the city's tax base, but it declined in the 1990s as the region was saturated with retail competitors.

The Lakewood site offered a potentially complex valuation problem for our company because the property had a split ownership. One entity owned the land and another owned the buildings. Yet this situation worked to our advantage because the owner of the ground lease offered a highly discounted price just to get the project moving. In other words, since the land was what generated the value of the property instead of the buildings, we could come to terms and acquire control of the property more easily.

Lakewood's existing lease and building conditions, on the other hand, presented hurdles to implementation. The center's four department stores were all anemic retailers by the mid-1990s, but the store owners continued to exercise long-term control over the property. When the original center was built, department stores had the clout to demand lease riders and extensive control over management issues. Today, this means that we can't change the color of the stripes in the parking lot without the May Company's permission and that Toys-R-Us has a 12-acre no-build zone around their store. These encumbrances severely limit flexibility in reworking a project and can hold up the process for years since the department stores have learned how to wait for lucrative settlements. Instead, we received a commitment from the city that they would use eminent domain to remove these encumbrances. Lakewood is now (or will soon be) home to several successful commercial projects such as a large, outlet-based "Mills"-type mall (made famous by places like Potomac Mills, etc.); the city decided to divert some of the revenue from these projects to help finance changes at Lakewood Center.

Villa Italia, site plan.

Central to this kind of long-term deal making is Lakewood's strong city manager and supportive council.

Two design firms competed for the renovation of the mall at Lakewood. The architectural firms RTKL and Alkus Manfredi each gave us two schemes, and we paid each of them to develop one scheme further. In the end, we decided to hire Alkus Manfredi based on the firm's ideas and creativity, as well as the chemistry of the relationship. In addition, we put together a citizens advisory group to be our critical link to and support-builder in the community. Eventually, we will conduct charettes and other meetings to insure local input and because we believe that the community can be a source for new ideas and solutions.

The new Lakewood redevelopment known as Villa Italia will be a mixed-use "downtown" for a suburban community that up to now has lacked a commercial center. After weighing different proportions of use types that met the needs of the local market, we decided that the 2.8 million square feet of new construction would include office, retail, and residential components. Another 1.5 million square feet will be dedicated to parking—more than half of which will be in garages. The street grid of the area

surrounding the site, which had stopped at the perimeter of the mall parking lot, will be extended through the site to better link the site into the surrounding community. The buildings in the new project will be largely traditional in design because other vocabularies would not work for this specific site and community. Our company is using more contemporary architecture in other markets in the region.

The city of Lakewood also has a large-scale plan into which our project fits. The site is adjacent to a recently constructed civic center. Across the street from the mall, the city built a new city hall and library to the rear of an older strip center (not the best solution but they had to get the projects moving after years of delay). On a street adjacent to the mall (a street that also leads out of Denver), we have asked the city to implement a boulevard project. We want to transform the fabric and density of the street to make it more dramatic. In addition, and perhaps more importantly, we want the city to zone a 400-foot setback for redevelopment. With a zoning change of this magnitude, it would be possible to assemble properties, add new uses, and dramatically improve the area. Continuum is confident that Lakewood Center will work at both local and regional scales and that both the mall and the neighborhood will prosper.

Two Malls, Kettering, Ohio

Marilou W. Smith City of Kettering
Andrew Aidt City of Kettering

Hills and Dales Shopping Center.

Kettering is a first-ring city of Dayton, Ohio, with a population of 60,000 people. Two older shopping malls in our area are both in deteriorating condition: the Hills and Dales Shopping Center and the Van Buren Shopping Center.

Hills and Dales was built in the southwestern part of the city in the late 1950s. It is a one-story, 250,000-square-foot building designed around an interior courtyard. The original center was home to retailers including grocery stores, furniture stores, and several large nightclubs. The 22-acre center is located at a major intersection through which, currently, about 20,000 cars pass each day. Although it is very close to a major highway (I-75), there is no local access.

Hills and Dales began to decline in the 1980s, and in 1996, it was sold. The owners tried to lease the center and also worked with the Planning Commission and City Council to create a special zoning district to allow for redevelopment. A new roadway and new landscaping were recommended by a county organization called Economic Development

and Government Equity (EDGE), which also would fund the improvements. Despite these efforts, the center is vacant and the city has been losing $150,000 in tax revenues per year.

The owners recently approached the city about buying the land, and after much debate in the City Council and considerable worry about whether taxpayers wanted the city to enter into the marketplace, we purchased the center for $1.7 million from our general fund and paid for demolition. We sent out a prospectus to sell the property, but the response was disappointing. We sent out a request for qualifications from architects to help us redesign the site, and there has been considerable interest. In the meantime, we're trying to market the site for sale and hope to develop it with a local or national developer, in whole or in parts.[1]

Van Buren Shopping Center is a single-story structure built during the late 1960s in the northeastern part of the city on a major thoroughfare. It was home to major retailers and a local high-end department store, as well as smaller retailers like Hallmark, a beauty salon,

Hills and Dales Shopping Center.

Van Buren Shopping Center.

Hills and Dales Shopping Center.

Van Buren Shopping Center.

and other services. It also has a bank and a post office and is close to a large manufacturing plant, a large apartment complex, and a business park, a redevelopment of a former defense-industry operation.

The Van Buren Shopping Center started to decline in the 1980s and is mostly vacant now, except for the post office, the bank, and a few small retailers. The site needs to be redeveloped, but there are property disputes and we are considering the use of eminent domain to settle the issue and redevelop the property.

The city feels that the site should be used for a neighborhood-focused, mixed-use development supported by the local residential community, but the current owner has been seeking to upgrade the property with higher-end retail. Unfortunately, a market study we conducted shows that such upgrading is not viable in this location as the area is over-retailed. We need to find other, more creative, community-based uses

for the site to avoid the drastic and costly action of demolition used at Hills and Dales. Subsidies are available at the state level for infrastructure improvements, or the city might be willing to trade the land for the right development proposal that included uses such as a public park. New housing is another option since there is great local demand, but the tax revenue generated from residential development is substantially less than commercial development.

With Hills and Dales, we were lucky that we could to acquire a property and absorb the cost of demolition to create a vacant piece of land. Unfortunately, we cannot do this again at Van Buren Shopping Center. As in many cities and towns across the country, we are left with the more typical situation of a semi-abandoned shopping center. The market is slow to see the opportunities in such places, but we hope that with continued publicity and some public subsidy, we can bring life back to these centers.

Demolition at Hills and Dales shopping center.

...successful development can take place only when local communities assume a stewardship role in defining and maintaining their open spaces, their streets, and their commercial infrastructure. This is perhaps the essential element in the repositioning of older shopping malls.

—Marilyn Jordan Taylor

III

Redevelopment: Projects, Strategies, Research

Architectural, planning, and design solutions for contemporary urban or suburban problems are never uniform. The built and unbuilt projects that follow draw from a wide range of proposals by architects, planners, and landscape architects for the use and reuse of public and private spaces. Not all the work is targeted for the suburban shopping center but is instead taken from a variety of situations and sites that highlight possibilities for reuse. The selected projects focus on the relationships among stores, homes, offices, community facilities, parking, open and public space, and local and regional infrastructures. The work includes both horizontal, low-lying solutions and vertical, land-use-intensive arrangements. This collection of strategies offers many lessons for architectural practice in general and provides a library of ideas for those looking for ways to rethink and redesign older shopping centers.

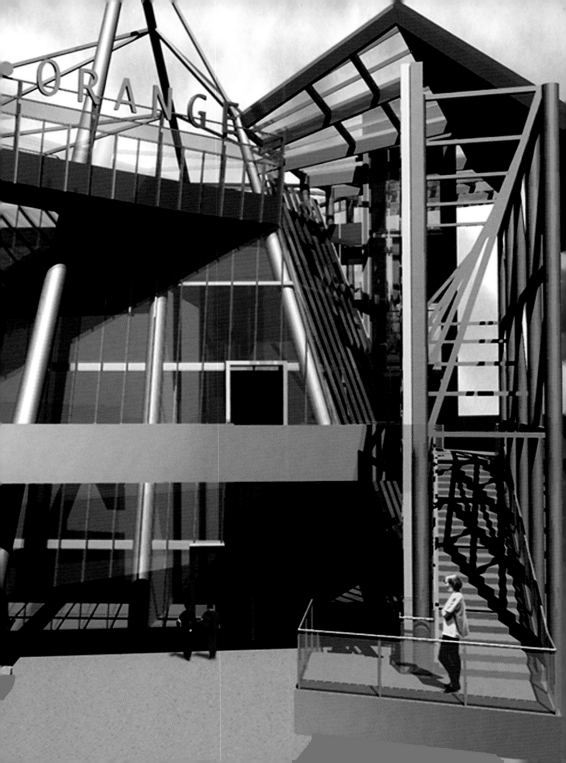

Urban Elements

Michael Rotondi RoTo Architects, Inc., Los Angeles

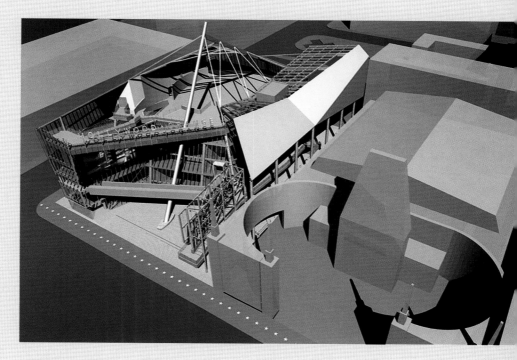

Mann's Chinese Theater

Hollywood Boulevard was once a very social place, filled with crowds strolling, going to movie theaters, eating in cafes or shopping. The boulevard functioned as a typical Main Street shaped by buildings and façades but it was also informed by cross axes of walkways, alleys, arcades, courtyards, and an occasional staircase. At the center of the busy scene was Mann's Chinese Theater. Visited by six million people per year, the Theater is still the heart of the district, but the average boulevard visit is now only 20 minutes. Half of the visitors are dropped off in buses behind the theater and have no sense of participating in the life or history of the street.

The clients have been a part of the Hollywood community for many years and sought a building that could add to rather than mimic or replace the cultural and architectural significance of the theater. The project links the parking areas to the rear of the theater, the courtyard of the existing building, and the sidewalk and street, creating a new set of relationships between the site and the existing building. It reinterprets the forms and social life that once flourished on the boulevard to create a new social space for residents and tourists.

Warehouse C, Nagasaki, Japan, 1997

Warehouse C at Nagasaki's new Motofuno Wharf is a transfer and distribution point for goods coming into and out of the port. The entire wharf, constructed in 1994, sits on a large landfill that projects 1000 feet into the bay. It is used by Mitsubishi Heavy Industries (MHI), one of the largest ship builders in the world, as well as the Mitsubishi Trading Company and numerous builders and industrial concerns. The building celebrates the port entry to the city and addresses the public prominence and role of shipping in the economic and social life of the region. The site also offers a unique vantage point from which the mountains, the city, and the bay can all be seen.

The location and size of the warehouse offered an opportunity to explore public uses and spaces alongside the private shipping functions that form the bulk of the program. The base building is an inexpensive and standardized concrete frame with dimensions predetermined by MHI at 1000 feet long, 80 feet wide, and 50 feet high. This vast roof length and area, as well as the views to and from the building, became the basis for a public garden called the Dragon Promenade. The additional programming was made possible by the money saved in the construction of the warehouse space. The publicly accessible promenade changes shape gradually yet continuously across the length of the building and forms part of what will become a larger pedestrian network.

Three Landscapes

Glenn Allen Hargreaves Associates, San Francisco

University of Cincinnati

Over the course of the 20th century, the University of Cincinnati has transformed into an inhospitable environment planned in an ad hoc manner and always oriented around the automobile. The campus organization and operation no longer contribute to the interactions that shape healthy student life. Confronting the necessity for more growth and a clear need to address the lack of spatial coherence, the university required a longer-term strategy. The heart of the reorganization reclaims a series of public open spaces and pedestrian pathways to unify the campus.

Devising a new site plan and reorienting the campus for the pedestrian required relocating parking to garages at the edges of the campus and diverting service roads to secondary networks. In addition, decades-old buildings intended for temporary use were removed to restore the original campus quadrangle. With these new spaces created or found, the geometries of the site plan could generate a series of linked and recognizable open spaces and quadrangles that together form a network for campus-wide connections. The pedestrian can walk from the old historic center of the university through a ravine and across the rest of the campus.

The Main Street Project, part of the overall plan, provides a series of urban spaces and links the old quadrangle to the new Campus Green, previously an 11-acre parking lot.

The new chain of green spaces leads to a major outdoor space called the University Commons, which invites the local community into the campus and uses land forms to create a variety of active and changing places.

Through a series of new or reclaimed public spaces, the plan of the University of Cincinnati is able to shift the perception of the campus and provide it with a network of places that promote community life.

Sydney 2000 Olympics

The Olympic site is well located at the center of the metropolitan region, but it suffered from many years of abuse. It had been home to the New South Wales State Abattoir, the largest slaughterhouse in the southern hemisphere; the State Brick Works, which created a massive crater; and the major garbage dumping ground for the city of Sydney. Adding to these complex existing conditions were the massive number and variety of sports facilities required for the games and the festivities. This situation forced the Olympic Coordination Authority to confront an amorphous spatial and landscape condition.

The site design for the Olympics needed to address the short-term needs of an expected 600,000 visitors per day during the games, as well as long-term, post-Olympics social life. The planning process involved the collaboration of the Coordination Authority, the city, public agencies, and representatives of surrounding communities. The design is organized by three overlapping parts. First, an enormous, linear plaza ties everything together at the heart of the site. Second, a landscape layer links the site to surrounding park lands, creates parks within the site, and ties the pedestrian system together. Finally, a pair of water features, one at the high point of the site and one where the site meets surrounding swamps and wetlands, celebrates the transformation of the site into a new town center for the western suburbs of Sydney.

The design ideas derive from the specificities and needs of the place. The geometries of the plaza come from overlaying the historical and current grids of the area, and the material colors come from the colors of the Australian earth.

At the northern end of the site is a manmade wetland built by relocating and recapping the garbage dump to create a series of interlocking ponds and marshes that join the surrounding landscape. It also serves as a holding pond for storm water runoff, and works as a cleaning marsh to recycle water that is then used to irrigate the rest of the site.

Louisville, Kentucky

The city of Louisville asked for design ideas to reuse and reclaim its abandoned and forgotten industrial waterfront. The city's rise to prominence was based on the Ohio River's shipping role in the regional economy, but the railroad and the highway shifted attention away from the waterfront. In addition, the highway physically severed the relation of the downtown from the waterfront and made it totally inaccessible.

The master plan reconnected the waterfront to the downtown. The city formed a Waterfront Agency composed of local agencies and public developers that used private and public financing to acquire 125 acres of land parcels along the river. Surface roads were rerouted around the park to make it accessible and usable. The new parkland carried the river edge into the city from the east end of the site as a bucolic rural park. After crossing under the freeway, the river edge is transformed into a 12-acre great Lawn that serves as an urban park for the downtown. The Lawn is highly programmed with playgrounds, retail areas, a plaza for the annual Derby Festival, and restaurants, as well as an amphitheater infrastructure. A 1000-foot-long fountain begins downtown, runs through the Lawn, and empties into the Ohio River.

Mixed Uses, Mixed Masses, Mixed Finances

Gary Handel Gary Edward Handel + Associates, New York

Lincoln Square, New York City

Programmatic invention is perhaps the most profound means by which new interventions and redevelopment projects can transform their neighborhoods. The Lincoln Square project is a four-phase, 1.8 million-square-foot complex that has been underway since 1990 when the city's real estate recession gave rise to the need for creative ways to program and tenant new development. The project was made viable by the incorporation of big box stores, cineplexes, or recreational facilities that had first emerged in the suburbs and were now looking to enter urban residential markets. These new uses dramatically changed the residential development process and helped get the projects financed.

The scale, shape, and street relations of the Lincoln Square building were transformed by the large volume needs of the commercial tenants. The building offers a new approach for residential building in dense neighborhoods by lifting the first apartment floor 150 feet into the air, providing excellent views and light. The base of the building consists of several levels of retail—one at grade and two below grade—

and three levels of movie theaters above. Other uses that bring life to the complex include a multilevel, 140,000-square-foot sports club and a dormitory facility for J. P. Morgan. In effect, the building is a kind of platform for in-town living, a "density buster" shaped by a large quantity of intense programming.

The movie theater complex is also positioned in an innovative way. The theater lobby faces the street, and its vertically oriented space is filled with people moving on each floor and up and down the escalators. The volume of the lobby, separated from the street by a huge glass wall, brings the hustle and bustle of urban life into the building.

The Metreon, San Francisco

The Sony Metreon complex is a new addition to the Yerba Buena complex in use and in form. The new 400,000-square-foot building evolved from the focus on large-scale retail and entertainment in a dense urban neighborhood seen in projects such as Lincoln Square in New York. The building opens up through a broad glass wall to connect visitors to the activities and sights of the Yerba Buena Gardens. The Metreon also has multiple entry points to increase the ease of access to the many levels of the gardens, as well as to Fourth Street on the other side of the building. As at Lincoln Square, inward-facing elements of the program are shifted to the outside.

A clear and consistent public policy framework was an integral feature of making the Metreon project possible. The San Francisco Redevelopment Agency (SFRA) and other community-based agencies have been working on the 87-acre Yerba Buena site for over 30 years. The agency has acquired the land through condemnations, government grants, and outright purchasing, and it uses the sale of public property to private developers to pay for capital improvements that enable the construction of public buildings. SFRA leases other properties to developers and uses the rents to subsidize the capital operating deficits of the nonprofit institutions. This model of public-private partnership uses the energy and enthusiasm of the private sector to subsidize public sector goals and has been remarkably successful.

Yerba Buena Gardens has become a new cultural nucleus within the city. Among the public institutions in the area are the Yerba Buena Center for the Arts, the San Francisco Museum of Modern Art, a performing arts center, and a children's museum; the Jewish Museum San Francisco, designed by architect Daniel Liebeskind, and the Mexican Museum, designed by Ricardo Legorreta, are in the planning stages. SFRA has also participated in the development of the Moscone Convention Center, three hotels, and upwards of 1000 units of housing.

With complex and mixed programming, as well as the clear and long-term participation of public agencies, redevelopment projects can become vital public places. The Metreon, like Lincoln Square in New York City, shows a definitive shift from traditional urban and suburban design approaches that internalize retail and entertainment functions toward an approach that makes these activities visible from the outside. This work trusts the viability of existing streets and places for access, density, and activity. The shopper or visitor does not need to be in a separate world but instead can participate in the multiple activities that shape urban life.

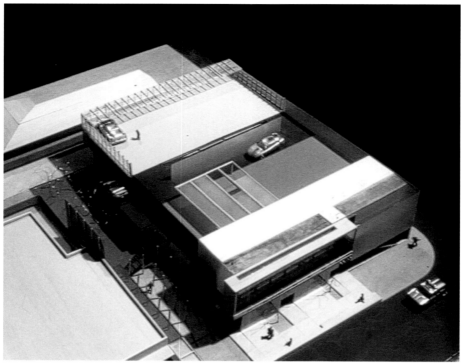

Stripscape, Phoenix, Arizona.

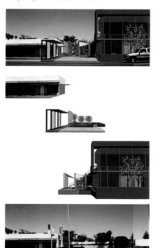

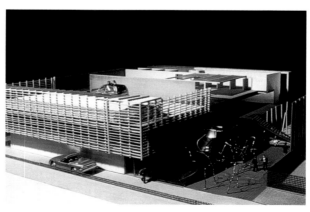

Reassembling the Strip and Building around the Big Box

Darren Petrucci Arizona State University and
A-I-R (Architecture-Infrastructure-Research) Inc.

Stripscape: 7th Avenue Corridor, Phoenix, Arizona

Stripscape is a revitalization strategy for integrating 7th Avenue, a commercial corridor in Phoenix, with its surrounding neighborhoods. It is based on a strategy of placing new elements into the existing structures and spaces of the commercial landscape. Potentially operating at the scale of a store or an entire mall, the additions of Stripscape form a public network by combining culture, work, living, and leisure activities.

In Stripscape, private commercial improvements by the local merchants are integrated with a public pedestrian infrastructure provided by the municipality. Existing underutilized right-of-ways, alleyways, utility easements, water retention areas, and required setbacks along property lines are reused as public and private pedestrian areas connecting sidewalks to service alleys, parking lots, and the neighborhood beyond. Uses along the new landscape infrastructures are "time managed," allowing public and private users to occupy the same spaces at different times of the day, week, or year.

Pavilions Power Center, Pima Maricopa Indian Reservation, Scottsdale, Arizona

The Pavilions Power Center is part of the trend in big box retailing toward increasingly large building complexes. The existing mall consists of a ring of buildings at the edges of the site composed of big box stores with long-term, 20-year leases, separated by smaller shops with short-term, 10-year leases. This project accepts the economic and marketing practices that shaped this type of shopping center but over time increases the building density of the site from 25 percent to 75 percent. The new elements that are added include housing, offices, and cultural facilities that are built on raised sections of parking structures with new small-scale retailing located below. Placing smaller stores nearer to the parking areas and the new public programming between the large stores helps to create a more pedestrian-friendly environment. In addition, the parking areas are transformed through landscaping into smaller-scale parking courts.

existing mall

Pavilions Power Center, Scottsdale, Arizona.

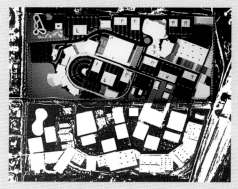

1996

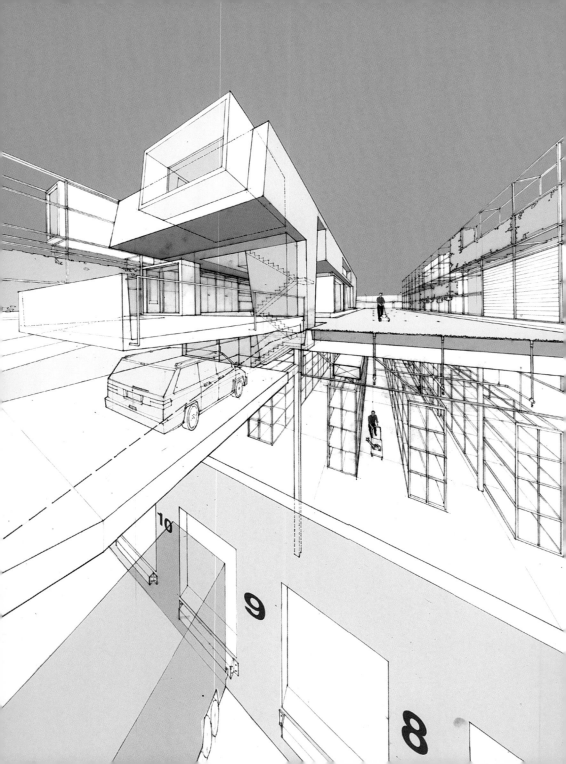

A Vertical Mixed-Use Suburb

Lewis.Tsurumaki.Lewis Paul Lewis, Mark Tsurumaki, David Lewis, New York

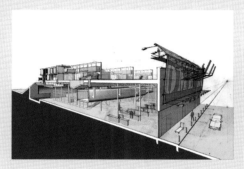

This project explores the impact on contemporary suburban culture of combining large-scale retail operations such as shopping centers and big box stores with the single-family house. The joining of these suburban building types creates efficient land use, sharing existing infrastructures, and reduces overall transportation needs while maintaining the patterns and social life of the suburb. Building houses on the vast roofs of retailing centers mitigates horizontal suburban sprawl and offers new opportunities for social interaction. In effect, the house and the store maintain their conventional uses, programs, and circulations while allowing new connections to the surrounding community.

The two building systems—the retail and the residential—share structural and service walls that also create the property lines for each house. These walls contain the necessary equipment for domestic life—appliances, cabinetry, fixtures—and provide usable areas between the houses for hedges, trees, and barbecues, reproducing a traditional suburban social pattern of overlapping private and social space. The new roofscape enables residents to enjoy a comfortable suburban lifestyle of indoor and outdoor spaces.

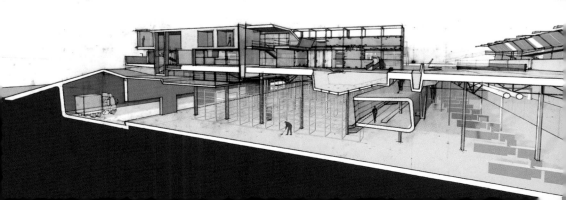

VMall: Vertical Density

SHoP Christopher R. Sharples, William W. Sharples, Coren D. Sharples, Kimberly J. Holden, Gregg A. Pasquarelli, New York

VMall, Flushing, New York

VMall packs a large, typically suburban program onto a small site in an increasingly dense neighborhood. Located in an area of New York City where retailing and commercial needs have not been met by typical development approaches, VMall introduces a mix of program elements the community needs and can sustain. The project houses a large neighborhood-based supermarket, five small restaurants, 40 commercial condominium offices, and parking for 200 cars. VMall also adapts to the specific features of the site. A 10-foot grade change from the front to the rear of the site connects a major commercial arterial boulevard to a residential zone. The programmatic and site conditions suggested a design that turns the typical strip mall on its side. The commercial spaces of the mall are stacked over the parking levels, and a vertical interior passageway is inserted through the project. This organization allows a variety of uses and activities to be seen at the entry and thus serves both pedestrians and automobile-based visitors.

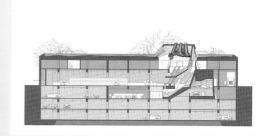

An atrium visually and physically connects the retail areas, the office floors, and the parking area below grade, as well as a miniature golf course on the upper level. The shaped surfaces of this volume display advertisements for the shops and act as orientation devices within the space.

Design Competitions as Catalysts

Rosalie Genevro The Architectural League of New York

Competitions, in all their various forms, are a very useful way to investigate alternative approaches and new possibilities in architecture and design. They are often used as an open-ended, explorative process, to elicit new ideas and perspectives when a building type is in flux or has become obsolete, or when an evolving form of social life has not yet become connected to a specific architectural or urban type. The reuse of older shopping centers raises all these issues.

Two very ambitious and fairly recent European projects suggest how complicated urban design issues can benefit from the competition process. In Ireland, a historic but dilapidated section of Dublin was slated to be demolished to make way for construction of a major transportation terminal. The city took years to assemble the land and, in the interim, properties were rented out at low prices to artists and other groups who eventually formed an organized community. Before the terminal went ahead, a competition was organized to come up with other ways to develop the area. The competition was won by a consortium of young architects, who proposed a precise, fine-grained strategy for the entire area, in which new buildings and outdoor gathering places would be inserted at strategic points. Design guidelines were developed for the reuse of the historic fabric as well. The community of artists and a local development corporation convinced the city to adopt this scheme and managed the development of the project. Today Temple Bar, as the area is called, is one of the most visited cultural tourist destinations in Europe.

Another competition of note took place in the Ruhr Valley, once the great steel producing area of Germany but long since in decline. The area was environmentally devastated by years of heavy manufacturing and mining, followed by economic decline and high unemployment, making for a very bleak situation. The state

government decided in the 1980s to create what it called an International Building Exposition as a revitalization strategy. In Germany, earlier building expositions usually entailed the construction of model housing, so the focus on an abandoned manufacturing district was unusual. A number of design competitions were held to commission development on specific sites. Among the competitions was one for a park called Landscape Park Duisberg North, which was won by the Munich-based landscape architect Peter Latz. Latz proposed to leave the industrial installations in place as ruins and to interweave them with newly designed public landscapes. Designed to be installed over several years, the park has groves of trees that help purify the toxic soil, a public plaza called Piazza Metallica (made from large steel plates scavenged from other buildings), former storage tanks now filled with water and used by the local diving team, rock climbing walls, and many other recreational and cultural uses. The abandoned site has been transformed in a very inventive manner, but without any erasure of its industrial history. The park has become extremely popular with the surrounding communities.

The lesson of competitions or design studies such as these is that they are not simply a way to solve a particular problem but can also be educational tools. They serve as collective investigative enterprises. They benefit architects by offering them a chance to explore ideas, sites, and conditions and also benefit the public. The process educates all the participants, informs and engages the public, and, potentially, makes the ground more fertile for higher aspirations in design. The best competitions raise awareness of the relationship between design and the life of communities.

IV

Development Issues
and Problems

The last word in shopping center reuse goes to those engaged in the financial, regulatory, planning, and political nuts and bolts of development. The participants in these discussions have extensive local and national experience in building, financing, and observing shopping centers in inner suburbs. Their discussion makes clear that there is no single formula for how shopping centers should be redeveloped nor for how the issue of public space should enter into the debate. Considerable breadth of opinion exists on the proper roles of bankers, lenders, developers, politicians, and administrators, as well as design and planning professionals. It becomes evident that design professionals and clients can only benefit from embracing and integrating these matters into their work.

For communities that depend on sales tax revenues for essential services, the problem can be a fiscal disaster. As the malls deteriorate, they often pull down their surrounding neighborhoods.

—Richard B. Peiser
Will Fleissig
Martin Zogran

From Shopping Centers to Village Centers

Richard B. Peiser Harvard University
Will Fleissig Continuum Partners
Martin Zogran Harvard University

There is no lack of underutilized property within the built-up areas of most American cities. Some of the best examples of underutilized proper-ties are the first- and second-generation shopping centers located throughout the U.S. Most of these properties are 20 to 35 years old and tend to be located inside the first suburban ring of a region. They typical-ly have been made obsolete by newer, more modern facilities in the second and third suburban rings around many cities.

Many older or abandoned malls could be converted to more stable long-term use if there were mechanisms to accelerate redevelopment. Such tools would help many towns struggling with large nonproductive properties that provide ever-decreasing tax revenues and are often located in highly visible sites within their communities. Conversion would also make available a significant inventory of large infill sites for denser and more compact development.

Many inner-ring shopping centers occupy relatively large sites for their locations, are typically adjacent to arterial streets that provide excel-lent access, and are often served by existing bus routes. The typical scenario for these "grayfield" or decaying malls is to slowly deteriorate over a 10–15 year period, while experiencing increased vacancy and reduced rents from a mix of discount retailers and backroom offices. In addition, surrounding commercial properties lose customers and often move to other locations, thus compounding the loss of activity, sales taxes, and jobs near the mall site. For communities that depend on sales tax revenues for essential services, the problem can be a fiscal disaster. As the malls deteriorate, they often pull down their surrounding neighborhoods.

Several fundamental hurdles need to be addressed in order to realize the redevelopment potential of under performing malls.

The Department Store Lease Encumbrance

Many existing mall tenants have leases that contain restrictions on changes to the physical layout of the mall without the tenant's approval even after the store has gone dark. In some situations, these restrictive covenants have stymied redevelopment for years. The larger department stores use their ability to block redevelopment in order to increase their leverage for future rent concessions, to protect their capital investments, and to keep competition away from the redesigned center.

The "Do Nothing" Scenario

In many cases, the owners are better off holding on to and neglecting the property, since it has already created incredible returns on their original equity investment made 15–20 years earlier. The preferred strategy is often simply to obtain rents that cover real estate taxes and minimal operating expenses. Eventually, another investor may offer cash for the land value of the mall, creating a substantial incentive for the original investor who has already depreciated the value of the building asset. The location and accessibility of many older malls make them viable candidates for offices, residential development, hotels, and new retail formats.

The Dollar Gap

Private investors make up more than 60 percent of grayfield mall owner-ship, as opposed to the insurance companies, pension funds, or real estate investment trusts (REITs) that own more recent malls. If these individuals were to give back the mall asset to their lender because of rising vacancies and lowered rents, a taxable event would be triggered, causing them to owe millions of dollars of federal taxes. A lender who takes possession of the property will want to recover as much of the book value as possible, which can often be achieved by leasing the property to backroom office operations or other uses, but this often draws out the devaluation process. It is likely to be several years before the property becomes available for land value only.

The Need for Aggressive City Leadership

Strong municipal leadership is essential in working with potential rede-velopers of older malls. This civic leadership begins with elected officials, city managers, and citizen boards, and extends to city staff, community organizations, and nearby resident associations. Using urban renewal powers and public financing to demolish obsolete structures, create new roads and parking facilities, construct civic or cultural buildings, and enhance the streetscape and pedestrian system are typical tasks for the public partner in such a project. The benefits of participating lead to the removal of empty and unsightly buildings, stem the decline of surround-ing activities, increase tax revenues, create new neighborhoods that offer a variety of housing types and employment, and establish a sense of civic pride in the community.

Public-private partnerships are key
ingredients in moving projects along.
Probably 95 percent of the projects
done by most lenders involve some sort
of public financing from a variety of
different sources such as loan
guarantees, tax relief, or other grants.
—Joseph F. Reilly

Roundtable: Obstacles to Development

Mark Falcone Continuum Partners
Joseph F. Reilly J. P. Morgan Chase Community
    Development Corporation
Ron Sher Terranomics
Donald R. Zuchelli ZHA, Inc.
Benjamin R. Barber Walt Whitman Center for the Culture
    and Politics of Democracy, Rutgers University

The transformation of declining or abandoned shopping centers is largely
an economic problem. The redevelopment of these centers depends on
the criteria, analyses, and the decision-making processes of financial institutions. At the same time, turning older shopping centers into viable and
successful public spaces also depends on how these financial players interact with governmental, design, planning, and community participants.
This complex and potentially volatile mix of players means that "doing
the numbers" for the public-private partnerships that are typically used
for large-scale redevelopment projects needs to be understood and inter-
preted by a wide range of participants. The following discussion among
three developers, an economist, and a political scientist provides a
detailed picture of the different priorities and needs of the financial community and how they affect the development process.

Mark Falcone

My company often looks at declining or closed shopping centers and we have formulated several criteria for evaluation that might be instructive in understanding how the redevelopment system works and how it might change.

First, an investor or developer needs to understand the asset base and the valuation the current owner has against a desired property. What is it really worth? Many of the shopping centers built in the 1960s and 1970s are owned by institutional lenders, utility companies, or pension funds. The more recent generation of malls are generally owned by real estate investment trusts (REITs). The earlier properties, and therefore their investors, are in trouble because newer, larger malls opened nearby and drew more customers. The early malls fought back by expanding, adding new anchors, or doing multi-million dollar renovations. In most instances, these changes did not substantially improve sales. An older mall in this situation might therefore be worth $70 or $80 million on paper, but the real market value of such a complex is substantially less, and in some cases, the market value is just the value of the land. This gap in value can take years to depreciated or write off, and no lender is going to accept this scale of paper value. In some cases, owners find innovative ways to draw out the process of decline, for instance, by putting back-office operations into an old department store. But often this is a way of postponing the inevitable asset devaluation until a buyer can be found and other investors will take the inevitable hit. Current evaluation is therefore critical for a new investor.

Second, an investor requires an evaluation of the encumbrances that come with a piece of property: existing leases, contracts, easements, and other arrangements that could reduce a developer's capacity to reposition the shopping center. At many older shopping centers built when the retail climate was different, the department store owners could demand lease and other land use concessions from the developers. Locked-in signage issues, no-build zones, guaranteed parking spaces, and other management rules create insurmountable hurdles in the reposition-ing process. Unless a developer can buy off these encumbrances or pay for endless litigation, municipalities need to use their public authority to make sure a troubled project does not sit idle as they wait for distant store owners to reach a settlement: even a dark store can hold up a project for years.

Third, if a developer wants to provide a project with civic space and activities, public reinvestment through bond issues, tax districts, or other methods is necessary. Only public money can move a project beyond what private capital can provide. In some instances, this could also mean that a city will need to direct revenue streams from one successful commercial or industrial project in order to jump start another.

Fourth, an investor or developer needs to see the commitment of strong municipal leadership. Part of the reason that older suburban shopping centers are in such a sorry state is that suburban municipalities have historically looked solely at the bottom line. There was no long-term thinking. Cities have more typically taken leadership roles and political risks and backed large-scale projects. Suburban redevelopment projects need the support and confidence of public agencies and elected officials.

Finally, everyone involved in redevelopment needs access to alternative ways of doing things and needs to exchange information and ideas. My banker recently showed me a two-level Kohl store, a design which I did not know about. It was very instructive. So in Colorado, I can sit down with another Kohl representative and show him a precedent that works. But this information must also be accessible to suburban planning boards and other relevant groups, which often don't have experience or background in reuse projects.

Joseph F. Reilly

In complex reuse projects the developer and the public official need to keep in mind what features of a development project would encourage the banker to provide financing.

The leasing of the project is vital and is related to both the construction financing and the permanent financing. Banks making the construction loan are not interested in the long haul: they want to be paid off at the completion of construction. By examining the leasing of a project, these banks try to determine if it can satisfy the secondary lending market or a permanent lender at the end of construction. In other words, the developer needs to have enough signed leases to carry the costs of building the project. Additional public space in a project does not produce revenue, so the financing becomes more difficult and in one form or another, the commercial portions of the project must subsidize the space. Lenders are also attracted by the potential for flexible reuse of property. Looking at the worst case scenario, lenders want to know what will happen to a project if it fails. A property will have more value to a bank if there is a cost-effective way to use a property in some other form than originally planned.

Community involvement and community ownership can be important in the underserved neighborhoods where older shopping centers are typically found. Community-based nonprofit partnerships or ownership have access to forms of public financing not available to the private builder. This kind of money can make a huge difference in moving a project forward and can ensure that the benefits of reuse projects stay in the community. Community developers can also make small-business loans and keep money local. Most large banks invest in third-party entities who use state-sponsored tax credit methods of financing to make these small loans. In recent years, the volume of tax credit loans has become cost-effective as well as lucrative and has helped many communities.

Jobs are also critical from a neighborhood point of view. The Community Reinvestment Act brings the banker and the community together to create construction and staffing jobs. In federally sanctioned Empowerment Zones, such as the Upper Manhattan Empowerment Zone in Harlem, the law stipulates that a certain number of jobs be provided to people from the community. The boundaries of these zones are often arbitrary, and eligibility shifts from one side of the street to the other; this on-the-ground situation can cause a certain amount of friction but, nevertheless, the jobs are created.

From a design point of view, there are several issues that banks tend to look for. In recent years, it has become apparent that projects that use less interior space and use the street for public interaction and gathering are sensible and cost-effective. Harlem USA, a new urban mall, is designed as a movie theater wrapped with shops on the street, and it works well in that particular location. Once inside, people in New York are very comfortable going upstairs or taking escalators, so you can also utilize second-floor commercial space. These features have made the project extremely successful, and street orientations have proven their viability.

Public-private partnerships are key ingredients in moving projects along. Probably 95 percent of the projects done by most lenders involve some sort of public financing from a variety of different sources such as loan guarantees, tax relief, or other grants. These kinds of subsidies remove some of the risk involved in complex reuse projects and encourage the usually conservative banking community to participate.

At the heart of any financial participation is the question of when and how to involve the banker. It may or may not be a good idea to involve a banker early. If you have the right banker with a long-term interest in a project, then early participation can add value. In contrast, a banker who is involved for just a two-year construction phase will have a minimal role. It often depends on the relationship between a developer and a specific banker or institution. Incremental approaches in which parts of a larger project are implemented separately or at different times are difficult for a construction lender to finance. If a bank has already originated a loan that can be sold in the secondary market or to a pension fund, changing the loan is not an easy task. Smaller banks that hold and service their own loans might be more willing to work incrementally, but many banks are finding it increasingly difficult to make smaller loans in general. The ongoing consolidation of the financial industry has aggregated deposits and decision making. In other words, there are fewer and fewer lenders who understand local market conditions. In this situation, potential borrowers are often left to the whims of the secondary market in which institutional lenders half-way across the country don't have the capacity to be sensitive to local needs.

Ron Sher

There are many ways of doing complex redevelopment projects but the confidence of the lenders is crucial. Bankers making eight or nine percent are not going to take development risks or allow incremental or partial financing to weaken their portfolios. Yet, in recent years, the secondary lending market has introduced methods of segmenting parts of a single project into loan packages called "tranches," each of which has its own level of risk and return. One package might be for the commercial space construction, another for a certain grade of tenant, or another for different sectors of the property. Needless to say, these deals are complex, but the net result is that developers can finance 80 percent or more of the cost of a project without their own cash. In troubled projects, this level of financing can make the difference between going ahead with a project or letting it lay empty. On the other hand, my organization avoids loans that will be sold into the secondary market because these kinds of loans restrict our need to make changes to the property and to run the project in a responsive and flexible manner. We'd rather pay a few extra percentage points to keep the attention of our primary lender rather than a distant, institutional secondary lender.

Perhaps central to convincing lenders to participate in a reuse project in a distressed or underserved community is the role of public money. The public sector has to guarantee some portion of the project to guarantee lender confidence. With the complex relations that result from big projects where the building, ownership, and tenanting arrangements are always in flux, only a developer who understands the needs of the lenders as well as the public sector can successfully structure a deal.

Central to these complex interactions is the flow of information and expertise. A quick survey of the redevelopment field reveals at least one major problem: there are great disparities in the way people understand how the whole process works. Especially in places where shopping centers are in trouble, very few people know the range of public and private market components that make projects possible. The roles and responsibilities of a municipality, the banks, and the developer are not always clear, and a project cannot depend on just one enlightened city manager or builder. We need to make the system work more smoothly. We need an organization that could transfer expertise to the city representatives, form connections with the retailers, and bring in the architects, landscape architects, and urban planners. We need to circulate case studies and take advantage of a huge knowledge base. Small cities can not afford the full range of expertise that large, mixed-used projects require, but if there was an organization to consult that could help educate their staffs on planning and development issues, cities could take a more proactive stance and offer more of their own ideas in repositioning older, distressed properties.

Donald R. Zuchelli

A thousand older shopping centers with a staggering 7 to 11 million square feet of commercial space will be taken off the market in the next 10 years. Many other centers will see their profits fall below a 10 percent rate of return, which would threaten any developer's equity. Developers are scared. Dead or declining malls can be retenanted, renovated with new types of merchants or community uses, or demolished to make way for entirely new uses. Ultimately, however, solutions to these failing places will come from the cooperation of public agencies and institutional lenders: the public-private partnership.

The first problem in the older centers is the dilution of the equity ownership since declining sales, failing leases, and empty stores make it difficult to pay down the debt, much less refinance. In many cases, the 30 percent equity originally invested is wiped out. Also problematic but rarely addressed is the hit taken by the small tenants in declining centers. Many have barely paid off their furnishings and equipment and have yet to make a profit, but in many cases the failing shopping center impels them to try to get out of their leases anyway.

The permanent lender has another set of problems. I represent various officials trying to revitalize a Silver Spring, Maryland, redevelopment called City Place, a five-story, 440,000-square-foot retail project that failed. The property is held by a good developer, but 87 percent of his leases are about to run out and none are being resigned. At this point, he is not paying down his mortgage. What happened next is very illuminating for studies of abandonment. Lazard Frères, the lender, simply put the troubled loan—a "turkey without feathers"—into a much larger and very attractive $500 million package and sold it to Starward, a secondary lender. Through this repackaging, Lazard covered up the $60 million loss of City Place by spreading it over other more successful projects. The loss got lost, so to speak, inside a package containing five good loans and three pretty good loans. Lazard later had to take back the problem mortgage, but in effect, they took back a $60 million credit for a future bundle so neither they nor the secondary lender lost money. They can wait for the troubled project to turn around and service its debt. Unfortunately, the original developer and the tenants who could not pay off their front-end loans were wiped out. Nevertheless, this situation shows that the bundling of financing and the leveraging of the bundle is crucial to freeing up buildings for repositioning.

City Place is also instructive for the ways in which public agencies and monies can affect a project. Among the earliest department stores built outside a major city, City Place presents some unique problems. The public officials have agreed to finance the historic façade restoration and to assist in the redesign of the street level to better accommodate new retailing. The city has also undertaken a new parking plan for the center. With these publicly backed elements in place, the redeveloper was willing to buy the $60 million property for $20 million and begin the process of recycling the building.

In general, public policy varies greatly from place to place and it is often difficult to know how elected officials, the general public, and the developer will define their involvement in any project. In many cases, the lender must mediate between public policy and the private developers' need to maintain equity and reasonable returns. In addition, the general public and many local officials often demand that developers rebuild everything with cheap leases and a high payment for the land. Any developer would just walk away. Instead, there needs to be a cost-sharing formula between the public and the private sectors, a kind of rational "public capitalism" that resolves democracy and privatization. In such a system, the lender, the mayor, city organizations, and the developer discuss, early in the project, the financial pluses and minuses, the infrastructure needs, and the role of each party. This kind of organization would give public policy a chance to really work.

On the other hand, the developer has to respect public process and citizen participation. There has to be stability in the political process and citizen support for the elected officials. Citizen involvement in redevelopment projects improves both the design process and the eventual product. In both cases, the positive environment helps elected officials make decisions. Ultimately, the developer has to convince the elected officials they can get reelected.

Also complicating most inner-ring suburban locations is the fact that as much as 70 percent of public services like police, fire, education, and parks are supported by nonresidential entities. The lost revenue from declining shopping centers becomes a serious problem for local governments. They have no capital except when the occasional brave or desperate mayor reaches into the city's operating fund. When nonresidential revenues shrink a few percentage points in any community, especially a distressed community, the tax increases that the residential population is asked to bear can generate considerable political acrimony. In extreme situations, some communities risk losing their autonomous, self-contained status as they face the need for county or state subsidy for essential services. On the other hand, with good planning, municipalities can use debt or bond financing, which pushes costs 20 to 25 years into the future. Public entities support the bond over the long term by small measures like sales taxes, user fees, and admission fees. From the municipal point of view, this is how complex reuse projects should proceed, but developers often fail to understand that public sector work requires long-term commitments.

At the opposite end of the spectrum, the federal government also offers mechanisms to move projects forward. Community Development Block Grants (CDBG) make available zero-interest construction loans for up to $60 or $70 million. These loans are U.S. Treasury backed and can completely change the economics of preconstruction loans, leasing, and placement fees. This can have a profound effect for abandonment and reuse projects because it can also help smaller tenant leasing. The federal grant can help start a revolving loan pool to assist tenants in furnishing their raw shell with lights, fixtures, and equipment. So public intervention can help the large- and small-scale aspects of reuse projects.

Benjamin R. Barber

There are several problems with the way public-private partnerships typically work in complex redevelopment projects. In many cases, a developer figures out how to deal with a big city bank and then goes to look for local businesses and, at the last moment, goes to the public sector to make the whole project viable through some kind of subsidy. The final result of the negotiations seems to benefit the big financial players: they make the decisions and take the profits, and the losses go to the public and the little tenants. The risk is spread across the public's back and the private side takes all the profits. Risk is socialized and the taxpayer takes the losses.

Most public-private deals have insufficient leveraging from the public side. Electoral support is crucial, so reuse issues must become part of the political landscape. Putting sprawl, development, and local business issues into the political landscape may not win an election, but getting a local mandate can strengthen elected officials in their negotiations in redevelopment projects. With zoning, curb cuts, environmental regulations, and control of transportation, there could be substantial negotiating strength. In many communities, the local vendors and businesses who are hurt by dying malls cannot go to a secondary market or a big bank. But these small businesses have many virtues: they are part of the community, they will stick around (unlike the big chains), and they're going to help win a local election. A strong local business community can strengthen public sector leveraging. If you get a group of local vendors ready to sign leases for a reuse project, the banks will be happy. So it's just as important to work from the local side of the financial equation as from the big lender side of the deal.

We need to put together a consortium of developers, state

planners, academics, architects, and urban planners that would be available to towns and assist in addressing failed malls. The financial and planning knowledge of such a group would be invaluable in low-income areas trying to revitalize a mall property and provide multiuse civic space.

Another method of assisting small and poorer communities derives from the kinds of micro-financing used by the United Nations throughout the world. Such financing makes very small loans—as little as $50 in some parts of the world—to start or enable local businesses. The costs of the loans are high since the businesses are typically labor-intensive, but percentages and rates of return are unusually high. In the United States, micro-financing of $10,000 or $20,000 for small vendors could mean the difference between starting a business or not. In addition, this kind of loan could assist a small vendor in getting an equity share of the building, in helping to develop the building, and in bringing a whole town around. These kinds of loans are high risk, and traditional banks are skittish about them, but they might dramatically improve the capacity of shopping center reuse projects to fill their spaces.

In general, all the players need to make micro-changes. The banks, the developers, and the vendors, as well as the public officials, have to make small adjustments to forge partnerships to make reuse and redevelopment projects viable.

A stimulating new vision is called for: one that can help rescue the failing centers but also help them to be genuine places in the older areas of our spreading suburban environment. We need to develop a deeper sense of how to achieve these changes, and to work toward guidelines for action. This is the challenge...

—Mark Robbins

Organizations

Bibliography

Image Credits

Contributors

Endnotes

Organizations

National Endowment for the Arts

1100 Pennsylvania Avenue NW
Washington, DC 20506
(202) 682-5400
www.nea.gov
The National Endowment for the Arts promotes design excellence in the disciplines of architecture, landscape architecture, urban design/planning, and historic preservation through grants to communities and nonprofit organizations. Applications are accepted in four categories: heritage and preservation, education and access, creation and presentation, and planning and stabilization. In addition to single-purpose grants, the Endowment offers special Leadership Initiatives that forge active partnerships with existing organizations to enhance the quality of design in specific areas.

The Mayors' Institute on City Design

1620 I Street NW
Third Floor
Washington, DC 20006
(202) 463-1390
The Mayors' Institute on City Design, an award-winning program sponsored by the National Endowment for the Arts and administered by the American Architectural Foundation and the United States Conference of Mayors, is a forum that provides mayors with the tools they need to create more livable, beautiful, and vital communities. At each meeting of the Institute, a small number of mayors meet for two and one-half days with a select group of prominent professionals to discuss problems facing each city and examine a broad range of ideas, precedents, and development strategies.

Your Town

c/o Shelley S. Mastran
1785 Massachusetts Ave NW
Washington, DC 20036
(202) 588-6000
Your Town assists rural communities facing a range of problems—outmigration and loss of jobs, rapid growth from suburbanization, an influx of retirees—resulting in damage to a community's vitality and sense of place. Two and one-half day workshops, sponsored by the National Endowment for the Arts and administered by the National Trust for Historic Preservation and the Faculty of Landscape Architecture, SUNY Syracuse, focus on the design process as a tool to enhance community understanding of new conditions. Participants include civic and business leaders, local government officials, and federal/state employees active in rural development.

Neighborhood Reinvestment Corporation

1325 G Street NW
Suite 800
Washington, DC 20005
(202) 376-2400
www.nw.org
The Neighborhood Reinvestment Corporation (NRC)—created by Congress in 1978 to revitalize America's older, distressed communities—supports a national network of local nonprofit organizations. The NRC creates and strengthens resident-led partnerships of lenders, business people, and local government officials to revitalize and restore neighborhoods in decline.

Urban Land Institute

1025 Thomas Jefferson Street NW
Suite 500 West
Washington, DC 20007
www.uli.org
The Urban Land Institute (ULI) is a nonprofit organization that encourages high standards of land use planning and development. The Institute conducts research, interprets land use trends, disseminates information, and sponsors a variety of educational programs. The ULI publishes a newsletter, *Land Use Digest*, and the magazine *Urban Land*, as well as numerous individual reports and books.

Van Alen Institute

30 West 22 Street
New York, NY 10010
(212) 924-7000
www.vanalen.org
The mission of Van Alen Institute is to improve the design of the public realm. The Institute identifies critical issues that confront the public realm, organizes tools and public-private partnerships to respond to these issues, and develops and communicates solutions through its programs.

The Architectural League of New York

457 Madison Avenue
New York, NY 10022
www.archleague.org
For over 100 years the Architectural League of New York has helped architects, artists, and the public enrich their understanding of the importance of the art of architecture. The League focuses on the aesthetic, cultural, and social concerns of architecture and the arts. Through its exhibitions, competitions, publications, design studies, and public programs, the League has a national impact, while at the same time playing a prominent role in the civic life of New York City.

Bibliography

Egan, Nancy. "Retail Roundup." *Urban Land*, April 2000, 68–71, 114.

Fickes, Michael. "Youth is Restored to Aging Missouri Center." *Shopping Center World*, September 1997, 40–44.

Gentry, Connie Robbins. "Changing Tenant Mix Adds Value." *Chain Store Age*, March 2000, 191–192.

Grogan, Bradley C. "Reaching Out to Redevelop." *Urban Land*, February 1999, 48.

International Council of Shopping Centers. "NonTraditional/ NonRetail in Shopping Centers," a list assembled by the Public Relations Department of the International Council of Shopping Centers, New York.

Kondrot, Keith. "Time for a Remodel?" *Shopping Center World*, August 1998, 58–60.

McCaffery, Dan. "From Mall to Main Street." *Urban Land*, October 1998, 22.

McCloud, John. "Coming Full Circle." *Shopping Center World*, December 1999, 42–56.

Phillips, Patrick L. "Remaking the Shopping Center." In *ULI on the Future—Reinventing Real Estate*, 18–25. Washington, D.C.: ULI— the Urban Land Institute, 1995.

"Putting 'Village' Back into a Regional Shopping Center." *Urban Land*, July 1997, 74–75.

"Public/Private Partnership Revives Urban Shopping Center." *Urban Land*, September 1997, 96–97.

Sher, Ron and Merrit Sher. "Developing and Investing in Local and Community Centers and Highway Retail." In John White and Kevin Gray, eds., *Shopping Centers and Other Retail Properties*. New York: John Wiley and Sons, 1996.

Urban Land Institute. *Developing Urban Entertainment Centers*. Washington, D.C.: ULI—the Urban Land Institute, 1998.

Urban Land Institute. *Shopping Center Renovation and Expansion: Selected References*. Washington, D.C.: Urban Land Institute, Infopacket no. 371, revised, 2000.

Vasquez, Beverly. "Denver's Mature Retail Market Evolves." *Urban Land*, April 1998, 71–75.

Image Credits

Contributors

Andrew Aidt has been the Long Range Planner for the City of Kettering, Ohio, since 1992. He is involved with professional organizations including the American Planning Association, the International City/County Management Association, and the Urban and Regional Information Systems Association. Aidt has presented his work at numerous planning-related forums including the 1999 National Planning Conference in Seattle.

Glenn Allen, ASLA, is a Founding Principal of Hargreaves Associates. This internationally renowned consulting firm of landscape architects and planners has offices in San Francisco, California, and Cambridge, Massachusetts, and particular expertise in reviving abandoned sites in a variety of locations. Allen is the Managing Principal of the Cambridge office. He was the on-site Project Landscape Architect for the Olympics 2000 in Sydney, Australia, and has served as Principal-in-Charge for such award-winning projects as the Louisville Waterfront Park, Parque do Tejo e Trancão in Portugal, and Candlestick Park in San Francisco.

Benjamin R. Barber is the Walt Whitman Professor of Political Science at Rutgers University and the Director of the Walt Whitman Center for the Culture and Politics of Democracy, Rutgers University. The Whitman Center has recently cosponsored the formation of the Agora Coalition to create model designs, foster creative cooperation, and broker public-private partnerships around the establishing of "mall-town squares" in commercial spaces. Barber also holds the Kekst Professorship of Civil Society at the University of Maryland and is the author of fifteen books including *Strong Democracy* (1984) and *Jihad vs. McWorld* (1995). His latest book is *The Truth of Power: Intellectual Affairs in the Clinton White House* (2001).

Margaret Crawford is Professor of Urban Design and Planning Theory at the Graduate School of Design at Harvard University. Her research focuses on the evolution, uses, and meanings of urban space. Her book *Building the Workingman's Paradise: The Design of American Company Towns* (1995) examines the rise and fall of professionally designed industrial environments. She edited *The Car and the City: The Automobile, the Built Environment, and Daily Urban Life and Everyday Urbanism* (1992) and has published numerous articles on shopping malls, public space, and other issues in the American built environment.

Mark Falcone is Managing Director of Continuum Partners, LLC. He previously served as Director of Operations and the Retail Business Unit at Pioneer Development Company in Syracuse, New York, and as chair of the Onondaga County Commission on Economic Development. He currently sits on The Nature Conservancy's National Development Council and Colorado State Board and cochairs that chapter's Heart of the West Capital Campaign.

Robert Fishman is Professor of Architecture and Urban Planning at the Taubman College of Architecture and Urban Planning of the University of Michigan, Ann Arbor. He is the editor of *The American Planning Tradition: Culture and Policy* (2000) and was a Public Policy Fellow at the Wilson Center in 1999. He is the author of *Bourgeois Utopias: The Rise and Fall of Suburbia* (1987) and many articles about urban history, urban design, and planning.

Will Fleissig is a Principal at Continuum Partners, LLC and an architect and urban designer. He is responsible for coordinating all planning, design, and entitlement activities at Continuum. He has been involved in developing mixed-income housing and has participated in a number of academic and research efforts focused on limiting urban sprawl. He has taught at Harvard University's Graduate School of Design and has worked with the Congress for New Urbanism, the federal Environmental Protection Agency, and Colorado University's Estate Center in Boulder.

Rosalie Genevro is Executive Director of the Architectural League of New York, an arts organization dedicated to the presentation of important work and ideas in contemporary architecture, urbanism, and design. Major projects during her tenure have included a series of design studies that address important public building issues in New York City, such as "Vacant Lots" (1988), "New Schools for New York" (1990), "The Productive Park" (1992), "Envisioning East New York" (1995), and "Housing for a New Century: Proposals for Arverne" (2001). Major traveling exhibitions she has organized have included *Hugh Ferriss: Metropolis* (1986), *The Experimental Tradition: Twenty-Five Years of American Architecture Competitions* (1986), *Renzo Piano Building Workshop: Selected Projects* (1992), and *Ten Shades of Green* (2000), a presentation of buildings that combine environmental sensitivity with design quality.

Gary Handel, AIA, founded Gary Edward Handel + Associates in 1994. The firm has become a leader in the design of complex, mixed-use urban projects and has won numerous awards including a *Progressive Architecture* Design Award, an American Institute of Architecture Project Award, an Architectural League Critics Selection, and the Project of the Year award from the National Commercial Builders Council. Prior to founding his own firm, Handel was a Senior Associate Partner at Kohn Pedersen Fox Associates, P.C., where he was responsible for more than 23 major projects in the United States and abroad.

William Ivey became the seventh Chairman of the National Endowment for the Arts in May 1998. During his tenure, the Endowment developed such innovative programs as Challenge America, Creative Links: Positive Alternatives for Youth, and ArtsREACH, and expanded its partnerships with other federal agencies, particularly the Department of Education. A folklorist, musician, teacher, and writer, Ivey was Director of the Country Music Foundation in Nashville, Tennessee, and Chairman of the National Academy of Recording Arts & Sciences before joining the Endowment.

Lewis.Tsurumaki.Lewis is a New York–based architecture and research partnership comprised of Marc Tsurumaki and twin brothers Paul and David Lewis. Lewis.Tsurumaki.Lewis recently participated in the year 2000 National Design Triennial at the Cooper-Hewitt Museum, and the firm was selected by *Architectural Record* (December 2000) as one of 10 young firms from around the world that constitute a new vanguard in architecture.

Kevin Mattson is Faculty Associate at the Contemporary History Institute and Associate Professor of American History at Ohio University in Athens, Ohio. Previously he was Associate Director of the Walt Whitman Center for the Culture and Politics of Democracy, Rutgers University. Author of *Creating a Democratic Public: The Struggle for Urban Participatory Democracy during the Progressive Era* (1998) and a forthcoming book on intellectuals who shaped the New Left, he has also written for a wide variety of popular and academic publications.

Richard B. Peiser is the Michael D. Spear Professor of Real Estate Development at Harvard University. He has blended his academic career with professional real estate experience, developing homes, apartments, and land in Texas and California, as well as consulting with real estate and governmental organizations. His publications cover a range of real estate and urban development issues including urban sprawl, new towns, real estate finance and deal structuring, land use economics, and urban land use regulation. He is the author of *Professional Real Estate Development: The ULI Guide to the Business* (1992) and is a Senior Fellow and Trustee of the Urban Land Institute.

Darren Petrucci is an Assistant Professor of Architecture at Arizona State University. He is the founder and principal of A-I-R (Architecture-Infrastructure-Research) Inc., a research and design office that focuses on the interactions and processes that shape the contemporary American urban and suburban landscapes.

Joseph F. Reilly has been with the J. P. Morgan Chase Community Development Corporation (CDC) since 1989. He manages a staff of 40 professionals within the CDC's Real Estate Lending Group, which provides financing for affordable housing and other community development projects throughout the northeastern United States. Prior to joining Chase, Reilly held several positions with the New York City Department of Housing, Preservation and Development (HPD). He currently serves on the boards of the Low Income Housing Fund, The Community Development Trust, and the Enterprise Social Investment Corporation.

Mark Robbins is the Director of Design at the National Endowment for the Arts where he has undertaken an aggressive program to strengthen the presence of design in the public realm. In addition to efforts to expand grant opportunities he has instituted new Leadership Initiatives including New Public Works, which supports national design competitions. Collectively, these activities have doubled the available funding for design programs. Robbins is an architect and an artist and maintains a practice that encompasses installations, curatorial projects, and teaching. He was formerly an Associate Professor in the Knowlton School of Architecture at The Ohio State University and Curator of Architecture at Ohio State's Wexner Center for the Arts.

Michael Rotondi, an architect and educator, is a Principal in RoTo Architects, founded in 1991, and a member of the faculty and Board of Directors at Southern California Institute of Architecture (SCI-Arc). Rotondi was one of the founders of this internationally recognized architectural school in 1972 and has taught there since 1976. He was the corecipient of the American Academy and Institute of Arts and Letters Awards in Architecture in 1992, and he was selected to the American Institute of Architects College of Fellows in 1997. Since 1999, he has also taught at Arizona State University.

Ron Sher is the Managing Partner of Terranomics Development, a real estate firm specializing in the redevelopment of retail properties, among them the Crossroads shopping center in Bellevue, Washington. He recently created the Third Place Company of which he is the Chief Executive Officer. The company, owner of Elliott Bay Books and Third Place Books, is devoted to creating retail places that foster community and improve the neighborhoods in which they operate.

SHoP/Sharples Holden Pasquarelli is a design firm with five partners whose education and experience encompass architecture, fine arts, structural engineering, and finance and business management. Founded in 1996, SHoP specializes in applying new digital technologies to the design, as well as the production and construction, of architectural and urban work. The firm's recent projects include a university academic building, a civic park, two public art installations, a museum, retail shops, and two mid-rise apartment buildings. SHoP was recently awarded the 2001 Emerging Voices Award by the Architectural League of New York and the 2001 Academy Award in Architecture from the American Academy of Arts and Letters.

David Smiley is an architect and an architectural and urban historian who teaches American urban and suburban history at Columbia University. He has published essays on urban history, sprawl, and suburbanization, as well as architectural criticism. His architectural work includes commercial and residential projects and campus planning in Jerusalem, Israel, and Washington D.C. He has also participated in urban design and planning projects in New York City as a Partner with the firm Design + Urbanism.

Marilou W. Smith, has been Mayor of the City of Kettering, Ohio, since January 1998. Smith was elected to the Kettering City Council in 1989 and served two terms including two years as Vice Mayor. A retired business professional, she is a member of numerous civic organizations including the United States Conference of Mayors, National League of Cities, Ohio Municipal League, and the Montgomery & Greene County Mayors & Managers Association, of which she is Vice President.

Marilyn Jordan Taylor, AIA, is Partner and Chairman with Skidmore, Owings & Merrill LLP. She first joined the firm in 1971 and moved to New York City in 1985 to lead an expanded Urban Design and Planning practice within SOM. She has also been active in airport and transportation projects, culminating in the founding of SOM Airports. She has been involved in extensive institutional, commercial, and residential work throughout New York City, and in additional projects as varied and far-flung as Providence Capital Center in Rhode Island, Celebration New Town in Florida, the New Jersey Center for the Performing Arts, Yongtai New Town in China, Canary Wharf in London, EuroDisney in France, and Sentul Raya in Kuala Lumpur, Malaysia.

Martin Zogran teaches in the Department of Urban Planning and Design at the Graduate School of Design at Harvard University and has his own architecture practice in New York City. He has worked for Rafael Vinoly Architects as a Project Architect for the Tokyo International Forum and for Margaret Helfand Architects as a Project Manager for the Swarthmore College campus expansion plan. His work has been published in *Domus, Interior Design*, and *Places* magazines.

Donald R. Zuchelli is the President and Chief Executive Officer of ZHA, Inc. in Annapolis, Maryland. This firm serves as the owner representative organization for an extensive array of retail space, office space, hotels, and residential units. He has 40 years of experience in economic development, strategic planning, and corporate management. He has been involved with projects including the development of a "town center" in Fairfax, Virginia; the location of the new Cincinnati Bengals' and Reds' stadiums; and the negotiation of the Mall of America project land lease. He is currently involved in the Urban Land Institute's (ULI) Leadership Council and the Executive Urban Entertainment Council.

Endnotes

Civic Space, Benjamin R. Barber

1. This essay is excerpted from "Malled, Mauled, and Overhauled: Arresting Suburban Sprawl by Transforming Suburban Malls into Usable Civic Space," in Marcel Hénaff and Tracy B. Strong, eds., *Public Space and Democracy* (University of Minnesota Press, 2001), 201–220.
2. Tom Peters in his *Brand You* (New York: Knopf, 1999), cited in Paul Starr, "Strategic Narcissism," *American Prospect* (March–April, 1998): 96.
3. Many developers have agreements with municipal transportation systems not to permit stops near their malls. Trumbling Shopping Park, in Connecticut, fought a three-year battle with the Greater Bridgeport Transit District to stop buses from discharging passengers near the mall on Friday and Saturday nights and in 1996 was supported by an arbitrator who ruled the mall had the right to limit service! In Buffalo, in 1995, a black teenager was killed crossing a highway to get to a mall in a suburb that barred inner-city buses from entering its property (though buses from upscale suburbs were allowed in!). See Jane Fritch, "Hanging Out with the Mall," *New York Times*, November 25, 1997.
4. Robert Reich describes this strategy of secession by which middle-class Americans try to escape the trials and burdens of the city by seceding into gated suburbs in which they buy private services with the monies withheld from public expenditure as part of a (public) tax reduction policy, thereby starving the public sector of needed support and worsening the conditions that justify secession to begin with; see his *Work of Nations* (New York: Knopf, 1991).

5. There are a few welcome exceptions. At the Stamford Town Center, mall managers hired youth social workers both to control teenagers and help make them feel welcome. See Fritch, "Hanging Out with the Mall."
6. This can make sense in certain parts of the country like New England, where a strong tradition of small town self-governance persists, and where hostility to suburbanization has strong roots. But in New Jersey or Ohio or central California, it looks merely nostalgic or, worse, indulgently elitist.

Antidotes to Sprawl, Kevin Mattson

1. Victor Gruen, "Introverted Architecture," *Progressive Architecture* 38 (1957): 204–8. See also Lizabeth Cohen, "From Town Center to Shopping Center: The Reconfiguration of Community Marketplaces in Postwar America," *American Historical Review* 101 (1996): 1068–71. On suburbanization, see Robert Fishman, *Bourgeois Utopias* (New York: Basic Books, 1987) and Kenneth Jackson, *Crabgrass Frontier: The Suburbanization of the United States* (New York: Oxford University Press, 1985).
2. Quoted in David Finkel, "Mall is Beautiful," *Washington Post Magazine*, December 10, 1995. Ironically, this mall was never built due to lack of community support.
3. Quoted in Ariel Sabar, "Providence Place: Will it Become the New 'Town Square,'" *Providence Sunday Journal*, July 25, 1999, A-1.

4. For reviews of the legal history and the issues debated, see Cohen, "From Town Center to Shopping Center"; Witold Rybczynski, *City Life* (New York: Scribner's, 1995), 209; William S. Kowinski, *The Malling of America: An Inside Look at the Great Consumer Paradise* (New York: Morrow, 1985), 354–9; "Now, Public Rights in Private Domains," *New York Times*, December 25, 1994; Heidi Gralla, "Public Access, Private Property: The Law, The Policies, The Debate," *Shopping Centers Today*, November 1991.
5. Nelson BOCK and Patricia Lawless-Avelar, Petitioners, v. WESTMINSTER MALL COMPANY, No. 90SC433, Supreme Court of Colorado, En. Banc. October 7, 1991. Rehearing denied Nov. 4, 1991.
6. Quoted in "Megamall Must Allow Protests," *Star-Tribune* (Minneapolis), July 25, 1997, 1A.
7. Maureen Bausch, "Mall of America Will Keep Barring Protests and Disorderly Behavior," *Star-Tribune* (Minneapolis, Minnesota), August 5, 1997, 12A.
8. See Juliet Schor, *The Overworked American* (New York: Basic Books, 1991).
9. Heidi Elliott, "Internet Still Not Home Shopping Mall," *Electronic News*, April 13, 1998; Susan Kuchinskas, "The E-Commerce Cometh," *Brandweek*, September 21, 1998; Danine Alati, "Retailing," *Contract Design*, January 1999, 57; Kim Komando, "On-Line Shopping," *Popular Mechanics*, November 1998, 40–3.

10 Edmund Mander, "Spate of Retail Bankruptcies Worries Industry," *Shopping Centers Today*, June 1999, 1. Steven Bergsman, "The Ground Floor: Slow Times at Sherman Oaks—What's Ailing the Malls of America?" *Barron's*, May 17, 1999, 40.

11 Alati, "Retailing," 51.

12 Bergsman, "The Ground Floor," 39.

13 George Homsy, "New Lives for Old Malls," *Planning*, May 1999, 20.

14 Sharon King, "Shoppers Get Awards," *New York Times*, December 28, 1998, C1.

15 John Melaniphy, Melaniphy and Associates, "Possible Solutions to Mall and Shopping Center Vacancies," photocopy in author's possession.

16 Leslie Kaufman, "Sony Builds a Mall, But Don't Call It That," *New York Times*, July 25, 1999, Section 3, 1.

17 See "NonTraditional/NonRetail in Shopping Centers," a list assembled by the Public Relations Department of the International Council of Shopping Centers (New York).

18 "Even City Hall Has Moved to the Mall," *New York Times*, July 30, 1995.

19 On first-ring suburbs, see Rip Rapson and William Morrish, "First-Ring Suburbs: The Next Generation of Community Policy and Design (University of Minnesota, Working Paper of the Design Center for American Urban Landscape); Herbert Muschamp, "Becoming Unstuck on the Suburbs," *New York Times*, Week in Review, October 19, 1997, 4.

20 "Crossroads Shopping Center: A Turnaround Case Study" (available from Terranomics), 20. See also Neal Peirce, "This Shopping Center Values Community as Much as Commerce," *News and Observer* (Charlotte, North Carolina), March 17, 1996, 22A; articles from the *Seattle Post-Intelligencer* at http://seattlep-i.nwsource.com/neighbors/crossroads/; and Ron Sher and Merrit Sher, "Developing and Investing in Local and Community Centers and Highway Retail," in *Shopping Centers and Other Retail Properties*, ed. John White and Kevin Gray (New York: John Wiley and Sons, 1996).

21 See Peter Katz, *The New Urbanism: Toward an Architecture of Community* (New York: McGraw Hill, 1994), 168–77; "Fifteen Ways to Fix the Suburbs," *Newsweek*, May 15, 1995.

22 "Failed Shopping Plaza Becomes a Town Center," *New York Times*, Real Estate section, December 20, 1998, 9.

23 Personal interviews with Mark Remsa and Bice Wilson; see also conference proceedings, Walt Whitman Center for the Culture and Politics of Democracy (Rutgers University) and the Institute for Civil Society, held in Red Bank, New Jersey, November 20–21, 1999.

24 Eli Lehrer, "Mixed-Use Malls Come of Age," *Insight on the News*, June 14, 1999, 23.

25 For more in-depth statements on these points, see Ray Oldenburg, *The Great Good Place* (New York: Marlowe, 1989) and the introduction to my own article, "Remaking Public Space," *National Civic Review* 88 (1999).

Two Malls, Kettering, Ohio, Mayor Marilou W. Smith and Andrew Aidt

1 According to correspondence from Andrew Aidt, December 31, 2001, Hills and Dales has been almost completely redeveloped, with two office buildings and public spaces completed, including a park in the median of the road and wide sidewalks with extensive landscaping. Kettering is in serious negotiations with a national restaurant chain and an office/retail developer for the remaining two sites. —*Ed.*